UNZIPPED

Dedicated to the two women I love

UNZIPPED

Proof that Power is the Ultimate Aphrodisiac

Scandalous sex secrets:
the very private journal
of a public servant

Anonymous

First published in Great Britain in 2006 by
Virgin Books Ltd
Thames Wharf Studios
Rainville Road
London
W6 9HA

A catalogue record for this book is available from
the British Library.

ISBN 1 85227 301 1
ISBN 978 1 8522 7301 9

Typeset by TW Typesetting, Plymouth, Devon
Printed and bound in Great Britain by
Mackays of Chatham PLC

ONE

'I have a carefully managed public face – and a very secret private life'

They say that confession is good for the soul.

If politicians have souls – and the concept is far from certain – then this book ought to benefit my chances in the afterlife immeasurably. I am, indeed, a politician.

I belong to the British Conservative party; the party which under Margaret Thatcher's iron leadership ruled our great nation for the entire 1980s, only to be reduced to a shadow of its former self, though it may now be on the mend.

Like many I began as a foot-soldier and got myself elected as a local councillor. Education, intelligence and ambition took me fairly easily on to the party's Parliamentary candidate's list. After many interviews in various constituencies, I stood as a candidate, only to see my hopes and prospects destroyed by the great Labour landslide of 1997.

Apart from my political activities, I earn my living as a business consultant, advising on the commercial implications and potential of public policy. Working as a lobbyist for certain companies, I network and deal with both MPs and government officials to persuade them of my client's cause.

In short, I am an insider, a very minor player amongst those who make the rules and uphold the value systems you have to live by.

To meet me, you would correctly guess that I am in early middle-age, but beyond that I bear remarkably few distinguishing features. I am neither fat nor thin, neither plain nor good-looking, neither ideologically left-wing nor right. In short, I have all the natural attributes necessary to succeed in my chosen profession.

In common with most of Britain's ruling elite, I read PPE – Politics, Philosophy, Economics – at Oxford, and went on to make a decent living out of my university contacts. And, like politicians the world over, I have a carefully managed public face – and a very secret private life that few people would ever remotely begin to suspect.

So why do I feel a compulsion to tell you about the world I inhabit? Because I have made a shocking journey of the kind these self-same politicians do not want you to make. Because after a lifetime in politics I have fallen out of love with the establishment and broken free from the shackles of social convention.

My story begins in 2002. I should be happy but am actually miserable, suffused by a sense of failure. I have acquired and done much that many people, perhaps most, would envy. But for me it provides little fulfilment. All my gods have feet of clay and I am yearning for a personal happiness which the world has so far failed to provide.

By the end I will have found it – in ways and places which at the beginning of my journey I would not have dreamed of. I will have turned conventional value systems upside down. And I will gain a deeper understanding of the philosophies I spent my years at Oxford studying well enough to satisfy my examiners, but without the real comprehension only experience can provide. Most philosophers are rebels and anti-establishment figures who prefer the company of thieves and prostitutes to that of the great and the good – as you will discover.

Come into my world.

TWO

'We have two very pretty girls . . .'

B rad is an American friend of mine who is both frustrated and frightened of his born-again Christian wife. The combination is an unhappy one which is why, one evening, when we are sitting in a wine bar close to Victoria station, he gets all excited when I answer his question.

'What are you doing after this?'

'Oh, there's this place I know,' I say nonchalantly.

'Can I come with you?' he asks eagerly.

Ten minutes or so later, we are in front of a door on a side street off the Wilton Road.

I am greeted by the blonde, Estonian maid like the old friend I am.

'I've brought a friend, though I'm afraid that he's here just for the view. He won't actually do anything.'

'We have two very pretty girls . . .' she offers.

'No, no,' insists Brad. 'I . . . I . . . just want to see what the place is like and have a look at them when they come in.'

4

Brad looks embarrassed, for I have effectively humiliated him. I feel little guilt as he lacks the courage of his desires. Contrary to what most people think, men have to work up the courage to have sex with prostitutes; the more middle class you are, the greater the barrier to overcome, for not only does society look down on the punter but so, in reality, do many of the working girls. They can be ever so sweet, exciting and compliant, but you know that they too can look down on you even though they need your custom.

But by this stage, I have long since worked out my own rationale and code. You will find out about it as my story unfolds.

In the bedroom, which differs little from any reasonably furnished room in any London apartment, I become momentarily disconcerted however, for something occurs I have long feared.

At many brothels, you are offered a choice of two working girls. This is what now happens as in walk Katya and Lara.

I am in a quandary. Over the many months I have been coming to this place, I have developed two favourites, each of whom I always choose when she is on. But now, for the first time, they are on together. It is not so much that I cannot choose between them as that to do so will be insulting, for each knows that I always choose her and it would be rude not to!

Meanwhile Brad's wide eyes and gawping mouth say it all. Both women are slim and tall, about five-foot-ten in their heels, and both are clad in transparent baby-dolls and thongs which leave little to the imagination.

I respond by walking up to where they stand next to one another, turning upon them a natural, infatuated, beaming gaze, kissing each on both cheeks, and then turning to introduce them to Brad, just like I would at the many Parliamentary receptions I attend. He is even more taken aback by the very normality of our mutual greeting for, as he uses me to dip his toe gently into the sinful world of London prostitution, he somehow expects it to be different from normal social intercourse.

I did at first, too. But actually it isn't. The requirements of good manners do not change because you are with a call girl. If anything, it's the reverse: they want a gentleman and appreciate you behaving like one – which I always do.

Brad shakes their hands whilst staring like some wide-eyed schoolboy.

'Sorry, I . . . er . . . just wanted to have a look.' They smile at him but for the moment his wife's and society's mores remain too strong.

The girls leave and the maid returns.

'Has he changed his mind?'

'I . . . er . . . no, I'd better leave,' says Brad. And with a wan backward glance at me, he leaves me to my heart's desire.

'Look, you know these are both my favourites,' I tell the maid. 'I can't choose between them, it would be insulting.'

I think for a moment, fish out my wallet and check its contents.

'Can I have them both together for half an hour for a hundred and seventy pounds?'

'I'll see.'

Moments later, she is back.

'They laughed, and say of course.' I pay her and she goes.

Katya and Lara enter arm in arm, smiling, and immediately take control.

'Strip. Lie on bed, on stomach,' says Katya, a Latvian blonde and the more assertive of the two. I do as I am told, as I will throughout what follows.

They sit on the bed, on either side of me. Lara, a Lithuanian with high cheekbones and a slightly wide face suggesting Asiatic blood, begins to massage my shoulders, while Katya attends to my legs, her kneading of my flesh firmer than that of her gentler, softer fellow Balt.

I explain how I couldn't insult either by choosing one over the other. They respond by chatting to one another in a foreign language, to which I comment, 'I wasn't sure whether your languages were sufficiently similar to allow that.'

'Like German and Hollandish, we understand one another.'

Soon I am told to turn over. Katya strips off her negligee and Lara follows suit. They now massage my front, Lara again at the top of my body, Katya lower down.

My own hands, meanwhile, begin to stroke the body of each girl, starting with Lara's belly and Katya's bottom. My own actions reflect my perceptions. Lara needs more foreplay, so whereas my right hand is soon delving under Katya's thong, I spend longer softly stroking Lara's stomach, thighs and breasts. For the perceptive man, paying remains about giving as well as taking.

By now I am rising and feeling that I am in heaven. My mind is switched off as I live entirely for the moment, one I know I will remember and treasure for ever.

Katya gestures that I should move towards her side of the bed and issues Lara with, to me, incomprehensible instructions. Their meaning is revealed as Lara lies down beside me. I gather I am supposed to enter her, which I do, with Katya still caressing me from behind. Once I am inside Lara, Katya turns her attention to my balls and anus.

The drink works its magic and, despite the exquisite sensations, I fail to come. Sensing this, and continuing her directorial role, Katya pulls me out, pushes me down on the bed, briefly manipulates me to bring back a full erection and then impales herself upon me whilst encouraging Lara to stroke and kiss my face and chest.

Still my body holds back. She has to resume use of the mouth before I cry out.

'Oh fuck, oh Christ, oh, oh!' My shudders tell her of her success.

She is pleased, because prostitutes, like all effective service businesses, want satisfied clients. She gets off me and, taking a baby wipe to the beads of sweat on her forehead, chest and shoulders, indicates to Lara that I should be cleaned up.

As we part, I can scarcely bring myself to break off from kissing and fondling first one then the other, while telling both that they are beautiful and wonderful and I adore them – which at that moment I do more than anything else in the world.

No one, least of all me, could have predicted that I would be the sort of man who would quite happily have sex with not one, but two prostitutes. What has happened to me and how did I get to this point? The following is my way of an explanation.

THREE

'I always knew he was really homosexual'

As I said, sleeping with hookers is for now some way in the future. What you are about to read is my sexual metamorphosis, from suburbanite to swinger, a journey common to more men than would care to admit it and particularly those men who for whatever reason opt for a career in politics.

My story really starts when I lost my virginity to a secretary in my first proper job after university. She took pity on me: in retrospect, it was a clear case of a sympathy fuck. She was eighteen, had been to an east London comprehensive, and was streetwise in a way I was not.

She invited me out for my 23rd birthday, told me that I was funny and acquired my virginity back at her flat, telling me it was a nicer birthday present than anybody else would ever give me. I always think of her with an affection and fondness.

The pleasure was repeated two or three times, during which I had my first taste of both giving and receiving oral sex. Women didn't shave in the late 1970s, but I enjoyed the experience for all that.

Then I met my wife. I'm going to call her 'H'. We worked at the same public relations company. She resisted me for five months, then decided my persistence deserved its reward, and thereafter we slept together more or less every night. I was bowled over, entranced, besotted and couldn't get enough of her, which is perhaps why I had none of the supposedly usual male aversion to commitment. I told her within 48 hours that she was gorgeous and beautiful and that I loved her.

'Don't be silly,' she replied. 'You can't know yet and I'm not beautiful, though I am the naff end of stunning on a good day.'

Looking now at her topless photo from that time I still think she's rather harsh on herself. The photo shows a delicately pretty, finely featured face adorned with a short, boyish crop of bottle-blonde hair. Blue eyes surmount a small, shapely nose and delicate mouth.

Her outfit of choice at the time – jeans and sweater – accentuated the androgynous look that was so popular back then. When I first took her home, my mother took one look, clicked her tongue, and said, as if confirming a long-held suspicion, 'I always *knew* he was really homosexual.'

FOUR

'You want to go out and bonk other women. I'm going to let you'

For most of my 47 years, I have suppressed my true nature.

This is how I became the real me.

One evening, I took H to see the film *American Beauty*. Kevin Spacey plays Lester Burnham, a forty-something advertising man with a status-seeking wife, Carolyn, played brilliantly by Annette Bening. Burnham is rapidly falling out of love with the American dream. About halfway through the film, there is a moment when Burnham appears to be about to make love to Carolyn, the only moment in the entire movie he comes close to doing so. For a few brief moments, she begins to relax and give herself to him, only to pull sharply away, saying, 'Lester! You're going to spill beer on the couch!'

The moment lost, they are back to vicious acrimony as he tells her that the sofa – upholstered in Italian silk and worth $4,000 – and her other possessions have become more important to her than the enjoyment of living. She has become joyless. What happened to the woman he married?

As we watched, I dug H in the ribs, leaned over and whispered, 'There you are, you see – *that's you.*'

I have since been told that many women would at that point have hit me. With great restraint, she merely murmured that surely, things weren't *that* bad.

But I knew that, for me, they were. Not much later, H decides to talk to me properly for the first time in ages.

We find ourselves at an impeccably respectable political dinner. It is the kind of banqueting suite where improbably large chandeliers shed rather too much light on fading, slightly-too-small penguin suits and blue-rinse hairdos – the kind of obligatory gathering that most Conservatives secretly loathe but are obliged to attend.

The after-dinner speaker is a distinguished Member of Parliament, but H and I pay her no attention whatsoever, nor any of our fellow guests. In fact, we are bloody rude for, after twenty years of marriage and to the complete astonishment of the other six people at our circular table, one of thirty in the large dining room, we do nothing but talk to each other all evening like a couple of newlyweds.

However, this is a conversation few newlyweds are likely to have.

We are still on the starter, fantail melon with a raspberry jus, when H says, 'I've thought about it and, you know, I do understand your reaction to *American Beauty*. You may not think so, but I've always understood you. I've thought about it a lot and I've decided you can, you know. I don't mind.'

I am bemused.

'Pardon?'

She repeats her comment, more or less word for word.

'I'm sorry,' I say, 'I still don't follow.'

She sighs, and puts it in words of one syllable.

'You want to go out and bonk other women. I'm going to let you.'

For once, I am struck dumb, so she repeats that sentence too before adding, 'I've always known you were going to do this. If you remember, I told you it twenty years ago, before we were married, and now I'm giving you permission: but it has to be on certain terms, *my* terms.'

And without waiting to be asked, she tells me what these are.

'You will be discreet, you will continue to respect me, you will not get caught, you will stay married to me, I don't want to know anything about it and you won't let the boys find out.'

This is a reference to our two sons, then aged sixteen and fourteen.

'Are you sure about this?'

'Perfectly.' Her gaze is clear and her words firm. 'You are going to do this by my rules, and you will not destroy our marriage or my family. But if you find yourself a twenty-eight-year-old . . . probably married or in a relationship and therefore not wanting to steal you permanently . . . but just to have some *fun*, well, you would not find me ungenerous, you know, ungenerous of you, that is.'

'So, er, what did you have in mind?' I am still in shock.

'That's for you to decide, because the one thing I'm not going to do is find her for you. That's something you'll have to do yourself. But since you ask, she'll have to be clever and she'll probably be taking her career very seriously, which is why she doesn't want a serious relationship. So a young professional in her late twenties.'

Two days later, sipping gins on our immaculate sky-blue leather sofa in our six-bedroom, semidetached Edwardian villa, I look her in the eyes, smile and ask, 'You know that conversation? Well, we'd both had a bit to drink and . . .'

I hesitate here for a moment or two.

'Do you remember what you said and, well, did you mean it?'

H is blunt in her reply. 'No, I wasn't drunk, yes, I know what I said and yes, I did mean it, because I've seen this moment coming for years.'

The second key that opens the door to my peculiar journey is seemingly accidental. Apart from my political activities, I am also a business consultant, advising on the commercial implications and potential of public policy. Professionally I mix with City types, bankers, lawyers, accountants and public relations people.

One day, I do one of these types a great favour. He had better remain unidentified in view of all the things I'm going to tell you about him, because he is a more significant public figure than I am. We'll call him Freddy, though that somewhat flippant name hardly does him justice.

Freddy is a political figure of moderate significance.

I approach him because I know about a piece of business worth a great deal of money but which I cannot personally deliver. I steer it in his direction, helping increase his already impressive income and career.

We begin working together. It is complicated, but essentially involves lobbying the government for our client. In practice, governments are like people: to get them to do things you have to persuade them that there's something in it for them. We plan to show ministers that certain changes will be popular enough to win them new support without losing it elsewhere. It sounds more difficult than it is.

It is about five o'clock on a wintry London afternoon when I leave the office of a Conservative MP. We have been meeting not in the Victorian gothic splendour of Pugin's

Houses of Parliament but in the ultra-modern Portcullis House where kindly taxpayers have paid over a million pounds per office to house some of our MPs and their retinues of secretaries and researchers.

So I have to take a short stroll past Big Ben, along Bridge Street and the east side of Parliament Square to reach the House of Lords and Freddy.

'How did it go?' he asks.

'Really rather well,' I reply.

Freddy is always understated, but the smile in his eyes is clear.

'He's agreed to some of the parliamentary questions I proposed,' I continue. 'And we tentatively discussed the Early Day Motion, though no promises on that one yet as he wants the answers first. But nonetheless a useful start. It should begin to shake 'em all up a bit.'

We briefly discuss tactics, drawing upon knowledge of Erskine May's handbook of Parliamentary procedure that I know back to front. Then Freddy says, 'By the way, I've been meaning to ask you what you want as a reward. Of course, professional rules preclude direct payment, though, if you are interested, I do have a suggestion.'

'And what is that, Freddy?'

'What you might call a very traditional form of corporate entertainment.'

'Meaning?'

'Attractive young ladies taking their clothes off.'

I accept.

A private bell by the Members' entrance to Parliament means that our elected (and unelected) representatives do not normally have the bother of summoning their own cabs. Freddy decides, however, not to avail us of this small perk, insisting that we walk along Victoria Street before hailing a taxi like everybody else. The reason for this rejection of privilege is very clear about three-quarters of an hour later, when we are deposited by a doorway in east London.

The large neon flashing name is unmissable from afar: 'Kaleidoscope' blazes above impressive black doors. The roped-off entrance is guarded by two dinner-jacketed heavies. Looking us up and down, they note the expensive City business suits and then one says, 'Evenin' gintlemen. You members?' to which Freddy replies that he is.

The doors are held open and we walk in, depositing our briefcases at a cost of a pound each – most things here are designed to part the customer from his money, though probably no more than in most places of night-time entertainment.

At the bar, which is a dark burgundy shade to match the rest of the décor, Freddy obtains not only drinks but a dozen or so laminated cards, the size of a credit card, half of which he slips into my hand. At a cost of ten pounds each, one of these shiny cards will buy us a dance.

We stand, drinks in hand, watching the ever more revealing gyrations around the floor-to-ceiling metal pole in the middle of the stage which occupies the centre of the large, semi-lit room. The woman wears a lacy black thong but nothing else. This allows us to see virtually everything as she grips the pole with her hands, lifts her feet off the floor until she is almost horizontal, forming a cross, and then opens her legs in a V to display most of her well-shaven and highly attractive pudenda.

I am mesmerised.

It is just the beginning. Two of the eight or so scantily clad women draped around the establishment now come up to us. Along with the skintight but easily removable garments each wears, one has high-heeled, black, shiny, thigh-length boots and the other high-heeled silver sandals held on by straps running up the leg from ankle to knee. The booted beauty turns to Freddy.

'Hello, Freddy, this is Jade. Who's your friend? I'm Willow,' she adds, turning to me.

Freddy offers a drink. Jade opts for orange juice, Willow for vodka and Red Bull®.

Within moments of the conversation starting, we seem to have paired off, I having acquired, or perhaps more accurately, been acquired by, Jade. She is a good six inches taller than me (though three or so of those are heels) with raven hair, a pale complexion and refined, symmetrical features. I am hooked.

'So what's your name, friend of Freddy?'

I tell her that and my occupation, and ask her about herself. It turns out she is Welsh, doing this a couple of nights a week as the easiest and quickest way to earn the money to study business management. She says she has a boyfriend who doesn't know how she earns her money and she lives some way away in south London, for no girl does this trade near where she lives, at least not if she's got any sense.

She also does it when on holiday, for if you are good-looking and exciting enough, it is a skill saleable in any major city in the developed world. After about fifteen minutes, she says, 'Would you like me to dance for you now?'

This comes across more as an instruction than a question and, without waiting for an answer, she takes my hand and leads me through a doorway draped with hanging silver beads to a separate area divided into cubicles. I sit down and fish in my pocket for one of the vouchers. We wait briefly until a new record begins and then she starts to dance. It is my first lap dance.

Her clothing is carefully chosen to come away with the minimum of interruption to her movements. She is soon naked but for her strappy shoes. She brushes her nipples against my lips, turns and displays her bottom, runs it down my crotch and then sits on the floor and opens her legs – all in one sinuous, continuous movement that is at once rhythmic and erotic. This continues in variations for the three and a half minutes of the record. When the music stops, she leans forward and chastely kisses me. As I watch her dress, we briefly resume discussion of her studies and then go back upstairs to rejoin Freddy, who has gone through a similar experience with Willow.

'Thank you, that was really nice.'

'I hope you'll let me dance for you again before you leave.'

The experience, the conversation and our politeness are all typical. I have already sought Freddy's guidance on etiquette.

'Oh, that's simple, treat 'em all like ladies, like you do your wife, and they'll like you for it and you'll get a better time because you are polite, unlike quite a lot of the men who come in here.'

It is good advice and broadly is absolutely what I have done ever since, not only with the dancers but with all subsequent working girls. Respect and consideration are at least in theory a requirement of the house. Heavies, the emperor-sized penguins at the door, are on hand to eject none too gently the overexcited, obstreperously drunk or otherwise objectionable customer.

Funded by Freddy, more drinks follow, and I steadily get through all my dance vouchers. I use them for blonde and brunette Eastern Europeans and an English black woman, as well as two further dances with Jade. All my choices are tall and slim – the classic modern model's figure – with the height difference emphasised by the length of the heels, which seem to be a requirement of the working dress. Most tastes are catered for, however, and the curvier, shorter woman seems to be the preferred choice of the majority of men, who wish to be able to look down on a woman, at least when she is in her stockinged feet. My desire to gaze upwards is a minority taste!

I'm curious about how much of all this money the girls get themselves. They pay the owner anything from £30 to £60 per night simply to be there and have to pay for their own drinks – which is why it is desirable that the punter buys – but keep everything they make beyond this. Clearly there are lean nights, but an attractive girl in demand can make several hundred pounds in one session, all cash in hand.

When we leave, a bouncer beckons a waiting minicab. Freddy negotiates a price for the round trip to both our homes.

Once we are moving, he starts talking about many of the lap dancers being students, making money to pay their fees.

'Labour's responsible. It's a side effect of their higher-education policy. When you and I went to Oxford, we not only had our fees paid, we also got maintenance grants. Now, it's impossible to make your way through university without running up thousands of pounds of debt, unless you're seriously wealthy, of course. What's the easiest way for an attractive woman to earn lots of money in a short time, with the minimum of effort? The sex industry. So, it's our gain . . .'

I smile at his analysis – a perfect illustration of the way a government's actions can have unforeseen consequences – and ponder the implications. Many of the women who service London's sex industry are generally better educated and more middle class than most people think. Of course, how far they go is a matter of choice. Some stick to lap dancing. They strip, allow a little illicit touching to increase the punter's excitement if they like him, but take it no further.

The clubs operate rather differently from the way people would imagine. There is more conversation and less sexuality but, also, temptation for the women to take it further. As I am to discover, many do.

When I am deposited at my house sometime after midnight, H is in bed. I undress outside our room and do my somewhat drunken best to avoid disturbing her. She acknowledges my presence to the extent of rolling over and entwining herself about me, but makes it clear she remains far too sleepy for the sex I badly want but – for now – will have to do without.

As visits to Kaleidoscope with Freddy become a regular experience, we discover the club's private room. The going rate strikes me as expensive, over £100 for half an hour of private dances with as many girls as you like, but he is paying. Jade is at the club but Willow is not, so I have to make do with her friend, Chloe, a slight brunette with a slim figure but breasts so disproportionately large and perfectly round that they can only be a surgeon's work.

Moreover, although the 'no touching' rule is somewhat relaxed, after a couple of dances it impedes further progress!

Jade senses our loss of interest. 'For an extra fifty pounds, we can do a lesbian show for you, if you like?' she offers.

Freddy accepts, so we recline on couches like two dissolute Roman senators with the girls standing before us. The action is rapid. Jade pulls her friend towards her and they begin to kiss with such evident enthusiasm that I suspect they should be paying us for the privilege.

I lean across and whisper to Freddy, 'I think they prefer one another to any man,' a sentiment with which he agrees.

Jade is the male of the pair with her hands taking the initiative, roaming over Chloe's torso whilst her tongue is manifestly penetrating Chloe's mouth. They break a little apart for Jade to unhook the clasp of Chloe's bra.

The breasts remain firm and solid as Jade manipulates them, before her right hand moves down to enter the matching thong. In fairness to Jade at this point, she half turns towards us and pulls down the garment so we can watch her fingers first rubbing then entering the prominent hairless mound.

They take to the floor and Jade goes from hand to mouth. Her lapping tongue between Chloe's parted legs causes shortness of breath and moaning.

There is a knock at the door. The half-hour is apparently up, though I suspect it has only been about 25 minutes. Jade lifts her head and calls out for a few minutes longer, before resuming at a brisker pace. Chloe sighs heavily several times before the couple break apart.

I realise that I have not even felt any stirrings, let alone actually become erect. The truth is I leave feeling bored, frustrated and seen-off. Ironically, I think Jade feels the same, for whilst Chloe has been satisfied, Jade has not. As we leave the room and the club I wonder whether they will continue later in private.

Freddy mutters, 'Jade is getting ever more mercenary. The value of the entertainment is not growing correspondingly. Time, I think, to move on!'

Which suggests he shares my feelings.

FIVE

'I can scarcely take my eyes off her'

On our twentieth wedding anniversary and at the age of 46, I fall ridiculously, hopelessly, head-over-heels in love with someone young enough to be my daughter: 'Angela'.

It is the birthday of Paul, 'New Labour' and therefore a political opponent, but also a friend. Together with a fellow Conservative, John, I join him and his party in a very trendy wine bar that's all late-twentieth-century Scandinavian minimalism amid Victorian splendour. On one of the sofas sits Angela, next to a man quietly showing all the characteristics of proud possession of this beautiful creature – they sit close, his arm around her shoulders, though they are facing and talking in opposite directions.

Do I believe in love at first sight? The answer has to be 'yes' though I do think it's conceptually more complicated than that. The initial reaction has to be reinforced by interaction to turn into love. Nonetheless, the attraction is instant and massive. When she stands, I can scarcely take my eyes off her, she has the figure of a model topped by the fine, even features of an English rose framed by long chestnut hair.

What Angela also has is grace and vivacity, expressed in the way she sits and holds herself, at once demure and exciting, controlled but constantly hinting at abandon, creating an overwhelming impression of depth of personality. I sit as close to her as the arrangement of seats will allow.

Our first words? I cannot remember, but they were banal enough, I am sure. But her impact on me – I remember that well enough. Three or four times in my life, I have met a woman and felt . . . not lust, but something much more complicated. Strangely, at that moment, pleasure and happiness have almost nothing to do with it. It is like a compulsion, a drive with all the loss of free will that those words imply. I felt it with H and now, for the first time in over a decade, I feel it again.

Over a period of time, John and I manage to manoeuvre the dynamics of the conversation and the seating plan, which changes as further bottles of wine appear, to the point where we have Angela to ourselves. She tells us she is in a gap year before going up to Cambridge. Not only beautiful and graceful, but clever: I am doomed!

As we chat, John and I show off. There is and always has been a natural rivalry between us. He and I leave together. I immediately turn the conversation to Angela.

'Well, she's a wow.'

'Too thin for my taste, as you know.'

'Thighs not chunky enough for you? I think she's spot on, and going to Cambridge!'

'Not a recommendation to me, at least . . .'

John thinks Oxbridge people generally lack common sense. I think he has a chip on his shoulder about not having gone there himself.

'. . . but I'll tell you one thing, though, that guy who she's with at the moment isn't going to keep her for long. She'll dump him as soon as she gets to Cambridge.'

As we part, all I am thinking about is how and when I can see her again.

Clearly nothing of this is said to H when I arrive home. As it is relatively early, when I ask for sex, she agrees, though as usual, somewhat grudgingly:

'Get on with it, if you must.'

Her libido has long been minimal, the sex we have once or twice a week being always at my request. Left to her, the frequency would be between three and six months.

Back in the office the following day, it is clear that seeing Angela again will be easy – providing I show patience. Paul is a networker and has organised a dinner to be attended by an assortment of political movers and shakers. They're all rather younger than myself and mostly New Labour, apart from a sprinkling of Liberal Democrats and a couple of Conservatives, of whom I am one.

I learn that Angela should be there – with man, of course, but that doesn't matter!

On the night of the dinner at the Cosmopolitan Club (another very New Labour venue), which is decked out in well-lit chrome, glass and pine, I await her arrival to see whether first impressions are confirmed – or whether it has all been my fervent imagination.

I approach her and we talk politics. She is a socialist and is going out with an aspirant Labour MP, the man John and I saw her with before. She seems genuinely interested in learning about the Conservative party so I tell her about selection and candidacy, all of which I can make quite entertaining to anyone interested. Suddenly she says, 'I had no idea.'

'Of what?'

'That you were older than us and had done all these things. How old are you?'

'Guess.'

'You must be forty,' she ventures.

'A bit more – forty-six.'

'You must be paid more than Paul – a lot more.'

'I'm not badly off,' I say with a smile.

'So how much do you earn?'

'That's a very direct question.'

'I'm a very direct person. A hundred thousand a year?'

'Oh, yes.'

She looks thoughtful, then asks, 'In the English civil war, whose side would you have been on?'

I hesitate. 'Probably the Roundheads . . . reluctantly, but Cromwell –' and in fact thought that for a supporter of New Labour, this should be the right answer. I am wrong and never finish my sentence.

'I wouldn't, you know. The Cavaliers are so much more romantic and exciting. Shall I tell you something – but only if you can keep a secret – you can, can't you?'

Sitting at the end of a table at right angles, we are by now leaning into one another. I am oblivious not only to the room but to the entire world except for her – and in fact there are spaces immediately around us as if our sudden intimacy is being subconsciously respected. At that moment, gazing into her eyes, the confidence offered, I would promise her the world and I know I am smitten, seemingly irredeemably though time will work its usual undoing.

'Yes, of course.'

'I'm thinking of switching – to the Conservative party I mean. I don't actually like Labour very much. I'm currently reading the biography of Georgiana, Duchess of Devonshire. It's wonderful. She's lovely. It's romantic and beautiful and I want something closer to that, for myself in my life. You could help me, couldn't you? I need a job.'

'What sort of job?'

'Oh, just something in consultancy or PR to fill in until I go to Cambridge.'

'I'll see what I can do, but actually I can perhaps help you in another way – confidence for confidence. You see, I've done some unpublished writing about the way the Conservative party really works. Shall I send it to you?'

'Yes,' she replies, 'I'd like that.'

I produce my card and she writes in a large, cursive but perhaps slightly childish hand, her name and home address. I know little of graphology but as I look at it, what strikes me is the combination of precision, elegance and space. I'm sure I've read somewhere that large loops indicate ambition – in which case she has it in abundance.

I leave the dinner in a sort of haze, compounded of drink and desire. No sex that night, H is asleep, so I lie awake thinking of Angela. I send her my writing the next day.

After a few weeks, I use directory inquiries to find her telephone number and speak to her father. I tell him I am ringing about a job for her – half true – and leave my name and number.

She rings back and we arrange to meet one lunch time in a wine bar near the office of a client of mine. A couple of hours before our rendezvous, the elderly male receptionist who doesn't remember names or recognise phone voices calls me to say, 'There's a message for you. She says she's left the country and can't make it.'

I slink away immeasurably disappointed, my grief a combination of loss and hurt pride that I have so badly misread the situation.

SIX

'I'm looking for a sugar daddy'

My phone rings; it's a female voice: 'I don't know whether you'll remember me.'

'Of course I do, I couldn't forget you.'

'Well, anyway, I've done it.'

'Done what?'

'Done what I said I was going to do – left the Labour party and joined the Conservatives.'

'Congratulations,' I say. 'You must be up at Cambridge by now.'

'Yes, that's what made it easier. It was a logical break point and I've joined the Conservative Association. And now I want to build my place and contacts, senior, powerful contacts within the party.'

She mentions wanting to work with a particular MP and wants to know if I can help out.

'I thought of you and wondered whether you could put me in touch or something.'

Although the MP in question is a friend of mine, something tells me to be careful.

'If you want to get in touch, the website is the best way. I can forward you the link. That's probably the best place to start.'

But what I am thinking is: shall I ask her out for lunch again? My father, a former soldier, always says, 'It's a good military adage, never to reinforce failure.'

'Look, do you ever come to London? If so, would you like to come to lunch with me?'

'Often . . . and yes.'

'So what dates can you do?'

It turns out to be convenient for just two days later. I choose a dark, traditional, wine bar near my office, the retro décor in contrast with the New Labour pine-and-chrome modernism I guess she is used to.

The lunch lasts nearly four hours and sets a pattern. When seeing her, I will be more or less taking the afternoon off.

What she says is surprising and not at all what I expect.

'I'm not enjoying Cambridge. In fact, I'm thinking of leaving.'

'What on earth for?'

'I'm not enjoying the work. It's not the fun I expected. The other students, well, they seem so young and the work gets in the way . . .'

'Of your social life?'

'Exactly. I come up to London quite a lot and I've always got an essay to do and it gets in the way. Also, I don't get on with the other students very well. In fact, the truth is I don't easily make friends with girls of my own age. I get on much better with older men.'

Then it all comes pouring out. She has a lover in London – not the man she was with when I met her, but an older, married man who has just set up his own public relations company and therefore doesn't have much money so can't

– or *won't* I think, but I keep that to myself – give her any. She can't afford the travelling.

'Have you ever made love in an office on the desk?' she asks unexpectedly.

'Actually, no,' I reply, feeling at that moment decidedly the less sophisticated of the two of us.

She enthuses about it – and him – for a couple of minutes before telling me how she wants to be a model, in her case, as I tell her, a decidedly realistic proposition. She is also wondering about lap dancing.

'I've been to Stringfellows,' she tells me. 'I've met Peter and he'll take me on any time I ask.'

Angela is Freddy's point about students and the sex industry personified!

I advise her, just as my father would, against precipitate action.

'If you're going to leave Cambridge, it should be for something specific not for some inchoate sense that London would be better – especially without money. Keep your options open – you'll only shut them down by lap dancing or posing for *Playboy* or anything which can come back to haunt you if you decide you want to go into public life.'

'I do want to be an MP,' she says, 'or something in the media: I couldn't bear to go through life, to die without being famous.'

'Well, if you want to be an MP, and it really applies to all the parties, on the whole, selection committees do not regard it as a recommendation for those who put themselves forward that they have either been a lap dancer or posed for a porn magazine.'

'Yes', she agrees, 'which means I'm looking for a sugar daddy. I think I could get one . . .'

This I don't doubt.

She goes on to tell me all about her home life: how her parents split up when she was in her early teens, so each has a new life but in the same city. She prefers her father; her mother she finds more difficult, mainly due to the presence of a new man who, in Angela's view, treats her mother badly.

By about four o'clock, we are the sole remaining customers, talking with easy intimacy. I kiss her goodbye and simply say, 'I'll think about it all and see what I can do.'

To my amusement, the next time I go there, just the following day, the barman says, 'May I say something to you, sir, something personal?'

'Yes.'

'That woman you were with, well, we just thought how stunningly beautiful she was, sir. Probably the most beautiful woman we have ever had in here.'

I agree with him, but that is not the point. He has never said anything remotely like that to me before, never assumed familiarity despite many months of patronage: it simply highlights Angela's head-turning potential.

I also realise something else. Normally a good trencherman, and with the belly to prove it, I have barely picked at my food and feel little inclined to do much more for the rest of day. Instead, later, I step onto the bathroom scales, stare at myself naked in a full-length mirror and am disgusted at what I see!

From that moment on, I can't get her out of my head. I function perfectly satisfactorily in terms of my job, at which I am, on the whole, rather good. I interact perfectly satisfactorily with H and my sons, indeed if anything I am rather more obliging than usual, *but I cannot stop thinking about Angela.*

So I ring her and, two weeks later, after one cancellation, we are again sitting in a wine bar, a different one which I have frequented on and off for 25 years: Mayfair, up-market, traditional.

The lunch-time conversation resumes pretty much where it had left off – except that we have both had time to think in the interim: me to accept her implicit offer, which I now try to do, perhaps too bluntly, and her to withdraw it! Oh, she likes me very much and still wants my help, but as a friend, not as a lover.

After this startling rebuff – how to lose a mistress even before you've acquired her – I retreat into a psychological parlour game which I have seldom found other than informative.

One asks the subject their favourite animal and colour and what they associate with them, and their feelings about water and being enclosed in a plain white room without windows or doors. These are Angela's answers as I note them at the time.

Colour: purple – regal, peaceful, sexy
Animal: cat – languid, seductive, independent
Water: the Mediterranean – warm, bright, relaxed
The room: claustrophobic – fearful, wanting an exit

The interpretation, which I give her, is that the colour represents one's self-image; the animal, what one is looking for in a partner; water, one's attitude to sex; and the room, one's attitude to death! Angela is delighted not only with the game but also with her own answers!

This over, she tells me she has to make a telephone call. She comes back with the elation of moments earlier having completely evaporated. Her eyes are watering.

'What's wrong?' I ask.

'The bastard!'

It turns out the married lover has just stood her up. With tears, the detail emerges. He has a wife and two young children and won't leave them for her. She is besotted with her lover and thinks she wants him on a permanent basis.

'So what do I do?' she finally wails.

Feeling a traitor to my sex and that I am going down roads dangerous for my own future relationship with Angela – whatever that might now be – I tell her, 'Most men, probably all men, will seek to have their cake and eat it for as long as they are allowed to get away with it. You have to put a stop to it and the only way to do that is to issue an ultimatum. You have to say that it's the wife or you. And if you do and he chooses you, you have to recognise the financial consequences, because under the divorce laws as they now operate, the man gets screwed by the wife with kids.'

'He won't leave his children.'

'How old?'

'One and four.'

'I don't rate your chances. The wife'll get the house and probably the working capital he needs for his business. You're asking him to give up a hell of a lot.'

We move on to her relationship with me and I explain about her message of months earlier and how I assumed she didn't want to see me. She recoils in shock.

'Quite the contrary,' she insists. 'I was really disappointed when you didn't ring back. I genuinely had to leave suddenly, but I wanted to see you and I told the receptionist to say that.'

'I'm sorry, really sorry but he didn't pass on the message properly. I didn't get any of that.'

'It's a real shame because you could have helped me through a difficult time, breaking up with my boyfriend and all that. I'd have liked you there and you weren't.'

During this part of the conversation, I get the distinct impression that getting into her knickers – a favourite phrase of H's – would have been rather easier then than now. So I repeat my genuine and heartfelt regret at my misinterpretation of her message. Later I ask her where she is going on to.

'I've got an essay to write by Friday for which I have done nothing.'

'What's the topic?'

'Why political leaders want to be glorified in art.'

'Right, let's start by listing who and what we should include.'

Taking pen and paper, I write: Napoleon and David, Hitler and Leni Riefenstahl, the emperors and Roman monuments, Justinian and Ravenna. The list is soon built, almost all of it coming from me.

'Now why would political leaders be linked to art and architecture?'

'Because it is the means to express and show their power and position to others?'

'Precisely. It delivers a form of immortality. Who would now have heard of Rameses, Nefertiti and Tutankhamun but for the pyramids of ancient Egypt – and popes who may have said they wanted to glorify God but were surely glorifying themselves?'

I annotate and structure the notes and give her a present – a book on how Conservative minds think.

'You're very special, you know.'

'And so are you.'

Later, she tells me the essay went down very well – her best yet.

At that point, the sensible man would probably have left it there.

I, however, am an idiot.

I realise that as, a week or so later, political commitments take me to her home city. I take a note of her home address, the one to which I mailed the book, and inquire at the office reception of where my meeting is being held whether they can tell me where the road is. Very helpfully, they give me a street map with the route I need marked in yellow highlighter. The address turns out to be an undistinguished and apparently not very large bungalow hidden behind an equally undistinguished block of flats.

Two reflections come to mind. To get from there to Cambridge is no mean feat, suggesting a UK equivalent of Clarice Starling in the Hannibal Lecter films, just one step ahead of poor white trash and desperate to escape.

And the second?

Is my behaviour beginning to verge on the obsessive? But as yet I am doing no harm, except perhaps to myself, so what the hell!

I sit outside in the car and phone her without telling her where I am. In this way, we arrange to meet in Cambridge. She chooses the restaurant, texting me: 'I've booked a table for 12.30 at Loch Fyne, opposite the Fitzwilliam Museum.'

I note the accuracy of the spelling and grammar, even in a text. The choice of restaurant turns out to be equally astute. As she sucks oysters, I eat little of mine as we catch up. This time, she is unforthcoming about her married lover, or perhaps there is little to add.

Of her family I find out more, especially when I tell her about visiting her home.

'You went to number twenty-six?'

'No, number six. That was the address I had, where I sent the book.'

'Oh, that's my mother's home. Number twenty-six is my father's.'

'And he's the one you're close to?'

'I have a close relationship – a relationship in which I talk about everything – with both of them but, yes, I guess I have a better relationship with my father.'

So she resents her mother moving on with another man. I decide that as a girl and his only child, she is a somewhat spoiled daddy's girl. Is that why she is quite so skilled at manipulating me? Interesting psychological depths, the roots of her ambition perhaps?

Now we discuss relationships and, because I have eaten little but drunk most of a bottle of Cava, I tell her again the effect she has on me.

'Look, I'm nuts about you.' I pause. 'I love you.'

'Why? What makes me special?'

'You're beautiful and clever. The whole effect is stunning, a real knockout.'

And I tell her about the barman in the wine bar, finishing with a rhetorical flourish, in the light of her lover's behaviour: 'I'd leave *my* wife for you tomorrow.'

Now there's an offer.

The only mitigation I can offer for this statement, which is the more outrageous the more ingenuously you treat it – what would I do if Angela actually accepts? – is that I had a pretty shrewd idea of her reaction.

'That's not what I want at all. Look, you know I like you a lot, I enjoy your company, I like you very, very much, but that's not what I want. I want you to help me and be my friend.'

And I am again twenty years old in Oxford listening to a girl called Camilla saying something uncomfortably similar. Nearly thirty years on and I have learned nothing, my seduction technique is no more effective, the relationship I seek is not that on offer. Yet I thought that was the proposition she had put to me. At least Camilla had never actually offered it. Or perhaps she did; I remember with great clarity a moment when perhaps body language had suggested what words had not. I will never know.

Going to Cambridge where Angela has, of course, a room, amidst an absence of rules (quite different from my time at Oxford), theoretically offers every opportunity to bed her. I suggest coffee in her room but am nicely but firmly sent back to the station.

Enjoying the train journey as I always do, I reflect that I am now beginning to notice also the small things. Though she smokes, she does not eat or drink a lot. There is a hardness, an almost ascetic quality alongside the desire to explore life. Is this perhaps because she thinks this is the only way she will achieve her ambitions?

By contrast, my working life is going well. I am now working with publicity-hungry representatives of the third party of British politics, the Liberal Democrats. Two of their MPs are prepared to be controversial and put down the Early Day Motion I have suggested.

On leaving, I seek out Freddy at his City office. In among the shimmering metal and glass of the surrounding buildings, it harks back to a different age, mahogany panelling and reproduction Georgian furniture evoking every institution he and I have ever known.

Business dealt with, I turn the conversation to what I am actually desperate to talk about: her.

Freddy is his usual informative self. 'The parental divorce in her early teens is probably the crucial factor. It broke up the happy home. It will have created an underlying insecurity which is where the ambition comes from. It will have wounded her psychologically, possibly to the point where she will never be truly happy despite everything she might achieve.'

'She'll succeed?'

'From everything you say, I'm sure she will, but there will always be an underlying unhappiness. It'll be subconscious. She certainly won't know the reason for her own discontent is that she feels betrayed as a young teenager.'

'Perhaps I could explain this to her.'

'Good God, no, that would be a disaster; she'd never forgive you for it. All of which, because she is also clearly clever, makes her difficult and dangerous, probably to be avoided and certainly not to be fallen for.'

'I think I already have!'

'Well, to get what you want will be far from easy and will require careful judgement with no guarantee of success.'

'I know. I'm ridiculous. At my age I should know better.'

'Ah, but whereas you say that, you don't mean it, because if you did, you wouldn't behave in this way. We have free will you know.'

'You've seen the Burne-Jones paintings, the *Tree of Forgiveness* and the *Beguiling of Merlin*. I am beguiled.'

He shrugs and smiles as he continues. 'On a practical level, two things. First you have got to impress her with your position and contacts, what you can deliver. Introduce her to one or two of the right people, but make sure you retain control of the contact.'

'Easier said than done.'

'Whoever said these things are easy? And then you probably need to arrange an attractive business trip somewhere nice where you can take her and lavish things upon her, though making it clear that there is only one room available and if she comes you will be sharing it. However, there is, of course, another alternative.'

'Which is?'

Freddy eyes me dispassionately. 'Just go and sleep with somebody else. Pay for it directly. In the long run, it will certainly cost you less.'

Freddy's words ring in my ears and later I decide to embark on an adventure of my own.

SEVEN

'We enter the bedroom'

As the traditional English black cab crawls its way through the rush-hour traffic, it takes us eastwards towards tower blocks and their rather more numerous lower-rise equivalents, badly built 1960s architecture, already the slums of the early 21st century.

My companion is an old friend I know to be adventurous, who becomes my guide for the next stage. We'll call him Harry. The taxi driver remains impassive as Harry gives the address but, as he drops us off at the entrance to one of these anonymous, down-at-heel, stained-concrete and dirty-glass boxes, there is a distinct hint of irony in the way he says, 'Enjoy your evenin', gentlemen.' The emphasis is on the latter word, delivered in exactly the way it had been at Sandhurst by the sergeants who train Britain's officer corps: the manner of delivery negates the word even as it is uttered. Like taxi drivers everywhere, he knows exactly what is going on and why two well-to-do Englishmen are being dropped in an area like this.

After negotiating the intercom and the stairs (the urine-soaked lift is mercifully not working) we arrive at our destination. My stomach muscles are knotted in a combination of excitement and fear as I knock. We hear the sound of a door chain being unhooked, a bolt drawn back, a Yale turned, and then I see a black lapdancer from Kaleidoscope.

'Hello, sweetheart,' she says to Harry, and he replies by pecking her on the cheek and simultaneously taking a bottle of champagne from his briefcase.

'That'll need another ten minutes to take it back to the right temperature.'

As I follow him into the room, I see another girl: she's about five-foot-eight, young, slim with short, bottle-blonde hair that doesn't quite extend all the way to the dark roots. She's wearing strappy black stilettos, white hold-ups of which I can see the tops, a largely red and very small tartan miniskirt, and a tight white blouse through which I can see the nipples of her small but perfectly formed breasts. Quite ridiculously, the phrase 'tits like champagne glasses' immediately comes to mind from Arthur Koestler's seminal political novel *Darkness at Noon*. One of the benefits of a good education is the complexity of one's frames of reference, which at once lend a sense of both romance and absurdity to so much that one does. (Later, when the girls are out of the room, I will voice the literary allusion to Harry, who laughs and tells me not to be so pompous.)

Concentrating as I am on the girls, it is a while before I take in the room with its chipped paintwork and tatty wallpaper, so old that if it were in better condition it would soon be coming back into fashion. It is almost devoid of furniture, a few cushions providing the only possible seating other than the equally shoddy fitted carpet and a hideous, imitation wood, chipboard display cabinet which I guess to be from MFI. But what the room lacks in furniture, it makes up for in electronic equipment: television, hi-fi, video and even a DVD; I don't have one of those yet.

The black woman looks expectant and without a word being said, Harry fishes for his wallet and hands over a wad of twenty-pound notes. She counts them, looks satisfied and disappears before the evening gets under way with a brief argument about music. The form of this is very English, for Harry and she each invite the other to make the choice: 'What do you want?' she asks, but Harry insists she makes the choice. This turns out to be All Saints starting with 'Never Ever'.

I love the choice; the working-class, mixed-race London group is particularly appropriate, for this represents the beginning of my escape from all the values I have been taught and now – supposedly – stand for. The very fact that the place is seedy and disreputable – and our behaviour as the evening unfolds will make it more so – is the repudiation of middle-class 'niceness' of the type my mother-in-law exemplifies. This is exactly and precisely what I am looking for.

Indeed, over the coming months, I am to develop a new frame of reference for everything I do; the more my mother-in-law would *hate* it, the more I *like* it. She would certainly not approve of Donna, for that is what my working girl is called. I love pretty much everything about her. She's twenty and now working out what she wants to do, having travelled around the world with her boyfriend. She is clearly very proud of this for, as she says, 'Rahnd this 'state, people stay 'ere all their lives, and I got aht.'

As this conversation takes place, she is half sitting on my lap, half lying on top of me as I sit on one of the cushions with my back to the wall. Harry is on another cushion close by, in a similar position with the black woman. I have taken off my jacket and tie. At first I am hesitant and passive and let Donna do the running as she begins to stroke my chest and then my crotch through the fabric of my shirt and trousers. Out of the corner of my eye I am watching Harry, who is running his hands up and down the black woman's legs, gradually getting ever closer to the brief, lacy, turquoise thong already being revealed by her rucked-up white leather miniskirt. My wife has always said that left to me she would dress like a tart; as in so much of what she says, she is entirely right!

I begin to follow Harry's example, soon reaching the naked flesh above the top of Donna's stockings. She is totally smooth and all I want in the entire world at that moment is to feel, caress and penetrate that beautiful flesh.

I hear Harry telling the black woman that she is sexy and beautiful and making small sounds of appreciation. It is clear that she is revelling in these compliments and I remember what Freddy had said in the lap-dancing bar: 'Remember, all women are the same of whatever class or type; treat them like ladies, appreciate them, show them and tell them that they are special. Do it as if you mean it and they will love you for it.'

So I begin to woo Donna: 'You're lovely. You have the most beautiful skin, so smooth and soft,' I say with complete sincerity, and I mean it for then and in all that follows my compliments will be sincere, a totally honest expression of my feelings at that precise moment.

We kiss and her hands are now feeling me. Up to this point I am aware that I have been largely flaccid: not any longer.

Harry, meanwhile, has disengaged from the black woman and is watching me while she briefly disappears. A smile of amusement is playing about his face as he asks, 'Enjoying yourself?' It is a question which needs little answer for the fear in my stomach is now gone and I cannot think of anything I have enjoyed more in twenty years; Donna is young, fresh, enthusiastic, positive and does not mind as my fingers insinuate themselves under the material of her red lacy thong to feel the smoothness of her shaven crotch.

And this for me is another first: my wife will shave her legs some of the time, but I have never in my entire life up to that moment felt a woman who is shaven fully. Until my first lap-dancing club, I had only seen them in magazines and now I am feeling her, running my hands over her nether lips.

'Like it, don't ya!' she says, but even as I answer with a smile the black woman reappears and we break apart as Harry opens the champagne, which we drink out of tumblers.

For a while the pawing stops and the conversation becomes general. I learn that it is the black woman's flat, that she has a child who is parked with a neighbour whilst we are there and that Donna is the younger sister of one of her school friends.

When the bottle of champagne is empty, arrangements are sorted: Harry offers me the bedroom with Donna. She takes my hand, pulls me up and leads me, the roles seemingly reversed with me as the shy virgin and her as the experienced woman of the world. We enter the bedroom, which contains a bed, a dressing table (again MFI chipboard but this time smothered in female make-up and beauty aids) and a clothes rail, burdened with garments.

Donna takes the lead in all that follows. She unbuttons my shirt, takes it from me, pushes me back onto the bed, unlaces my shoes, undoes my flies and I raise my hips as she takes off my trousers and underpants in one deft movement. Her own skirt and blouse follow as I watch, but she keeps on the hold-ups and thong as she climbs on top of me.

As I am now erect, she briefly disappears to the dressing table for two packets, one is a condom, which is put on me, while the other is a lubricant, which she smears across her crotch. She kneels over me, puts my penis inside her and then begins to make encouraging noises, interspersed with phrases and words like 'Yeah!' and 'Ain't that good!'

It does not take very long before I come, rather noisily, and she warns me, 'Not so loud!' That's another theme that will recur in the months ahead.

She wipes me with a baby wipe and offers me the bathroom. When I come out, she points me back to the living room, as I gather that Harry and the black girl are already making use of the bed, whilst she goes to use the bathroom herself.

I sit on a cushion for a few minutes before she reappears wearing only a thong – but that is still one garment more than I have. No words are now exchanged as she puts on some more music, which this time I don't recognise.

It is not long before Harry and the black woman emerge. More champagne is produced, then he asks me if I want to swap partners. It's a question that invites the answer 'yes'. He tells me to go first again – 'You've had the longer recovery time, after all' – and I'm soon being masturbated by the black woman. This time it all takes rather longer, giving me time to note that her body is larger but firmer than that of Donna.

When it's over I take my clothes with me so am able to dress as I wait. Truth be told, all I want to do now is leave. I feel a certain fear at what I've done and where I am. I am frightened of somehow being caught, though in reality the chances of this are negligible, and I simply want to get out as quickly as possible.

In the taxi back, Harry asks me whether I have enjoyed it and suggests the broad grin on my face appears to answer the question. I tell him it has been one of the best experiences of my entire life.

It has also increased by about 30 per cent the total number of women I have ever had.

EIGHT

'Variety is the spice of life'

It is a couple of weeks later, and the contrast could not be greater in every way. Harry and I begin in the inevitable City wine bar, part of the Davy's chain.

Over the first bottle we discuss business; we are halfway through the second before I somewhat too casually inquire, 'Any chance of repeating last Friday week?'

He smiles enigmatically. 'Oh, variety is the spice of life and all that, so perhaps not exactly – but I don't think you'll be disappointed.'

But I will have to contain my impatience as the conversation moves to other topics.

Two days later he rings to ask whether I might be free the coming Thursday. I am.

We meet in the lobby of an expensive London hotel; the champagne is already on the table.

'They should arrive in fifteen minutes or so,' says Harry. I immediately sense that these working girls will be a very different proposition from their predecessors. Nor am I wrong. They are both clearly quite a bit older but also a lot more sophisticated.

One has blonde hair (no roots showing this time) cut in a Louise Brooks bob, and is tall and model-slim. Her face is beautifully made up, though less fine-featured than I expect. Her name is Jean, she tells me as she sits down, her long black pencil skirt falling open via a waist-high slit to reveal a tantalising glimpse of what I see to be a stocking-clad leg from the suspender-belt fastening just visible at the top. I prefer her, but judging by past experience, both might be on offer.

Her companion, a brunette called Vivienne, is of similar height but somewhat curvier and plumper. Again the features are heavier than I would anticipate but the beautiful presentation, a classic little black dress with silver accessories, more than compensates.

Harry buys more champagne and the conversation flows, covering the usual inanities: the relative ease of getting there, the headlines in that day's *Standard* and, less usual this, the prospects for the new rugby season, a topic in which the girls are more interested than most women of my acquaintance.

'Time to go upstairs,' I say as the second bottle is drained.

Expensive, modern hotel suites are similar the world over. We might as well have been in Frankfurt or New York for all the originality of the rooms we enter half a dozen floors above. I note that no money changes hands and, as the girls have conveniently disappeared to the bathroom together, I ask Harry about this.

'A credit card in advance,' he explains. 'Now listen, how do you want to do this? We can either each have one in separate rooms, that's why I got a suite, though only one of us can then have a bed, or we can all four do it together. The choice is yours.'

I am flummoxed, although I generally try to fit in with other people's wishes, especially when they are good enough to pay.

'I don't know . . . do you have a preference?'

'Oh, I think it might be rather fun to watch one another and I know the girls don't mind, but I don't want to embarrass you so it's entirely your choice.'

'Well, fine – together, then, I think.'

He goes to the fridge for what is now our third bottle of champagne as the girls reappear. Although the action is to be communal, clearly initial pairing is necessary and I find myself heading to the bedroom hand in hand with the blonde.

Inside is a king-size bed. Shoes, suits, skirts and dresses are removed before we lie as two couples, beginning the process of exploring one another's bodies.

'You must work out?' I suggest to Jean, who responds by turning to Vivienne.

'He thinks I work out!'

Vivienne replies on Jean's behalf: 'She does, darling, she does and very pretty it can be to watch, too!'

By this stage I have, much to my pleasure, lost about two stone and am no longer quite as disgusted by my naked reflection though I still feel plumper than I wish.

'You know, I really should join a gym myself.'

'Do, darling, do, it'll do you the world of good,' Jean replies, pinching a lump of my spare tyre.

Harry meanwhile has been doing less talking but is making the appreciative 'mmm' noise I remember from last time. Vivienne seems pleased, for she has removed his last vestiges of clothing and is herself now dressed only in stockings and suspenders, both black. Interestingly, her nether regions are by no means clean-shaven and neither (I am about to discover) are Jean's. As I will realise over the months that follow, this amount of hair is most unusual amongst working girls.

Without entirely ceasing to caress one another, Jean and I turn and watch as Harry takes Vivienne in the classic missionary position.

'Our turn now, darling!' Jean tells me.

After some pleasant mutual manual stimulation, though she is more than a little reluctant to allow my fingers too far inside, I enter her – condom encased, as always – and begin to thrust, at which point I realise my mistake.

I have allowed myself to have rather too much of three bottles of champagne.

'Never mind, darling, I'm sure we can have a pleasant enough time,' she assures me, and we do, although – despite also entering Vivienne – it is one occasion when I am unable to orgasm.

As I am relaxing, I notice something disturbing.

I see that Jean – and then on closer inspection *both* of our ladies – appear to have an Adam's apple. So here I am, a straight Conservative guy of relatively limited sexual experience, who has just bedded two blokes.

Initially, I am a little queasy.

But when I think about it, I am not nearly as shocked as I would have expected. I have always believed that the activities of consenting adults behind closed doors are entirely a matter for them. Actually, my overwhelming feeling is of curiosity satisfied. I have added transsexuals to my repertoire and, in truth, found the physical experience little or no different from going to bed with any other woman.

I think I would take the same view even if I were less inebriated.

The one difference perhaps lies in their decision to remain hairier, possibly a result of nervousness about the visual appearance of their many thousands of pounds' worth of surgery.

I lack the courage at the time to ask them directly about the other dimension that interests me; their level of sexual enjoyment with their capacity for orgasm presumably removed. As we talk on the way home, it turns out that Harry has sought the answer to the same question. Done by an expert surgeon, the flesh of the penis is retained and inverted to form the artificial vagina. In particular, the most sensitive part, the frenulum or skin on the underside where the head meets the shaft – what any expert in masturbation or fellatio knows to concentrate on – is used to form an artificial G-spot well inside. Thus although unable to orgasm in the conventional sense, a male-to-female trans-sexual can have a highly charged erotic experience.

I clearly provided this sufficiently for Harry to tell me on a couple of subsequent occasions that Jean has inquired after me. Much as I enjoyed it, however, I decide that I am more interested in those born as women, especially if I am going to be doing the paying.

NINE

'My friend informs me that he wishes to be buggered'

I decide to take another friend out to celebrate the Early Day Motion reaching 100 signatures, a milestone on the way to my target of 250.

It amazed me that once my sexual proclivities were out in the open, some of the friends and acquaintances that I had suddenly became much more open about their own tastes. This friend, who I had met briefly at a party some years earlier and had remained in touch with, has warned me in advance that he was about to reveal aspects of himself that he had never revealed to anyone else, and he is not taking the decision to involve me lightly. Nonetheless he feels our friendship is close enough for me to learn certain of his tastes, and he thinks I might find the experience rather entertaining.

The location is an undistinguished apartment block in Covent Garden. The rooms are all drapes, incense, and semidarkness, and the lighting is hidden to cast shadows. The result is that the individual concerned remains shadowy to me even now. What I do remember with the greatest clarity and sharpness is the action.

As we arrive, our hostess, a mixed-race, African-English woman, is wearing a dressing gown. When this is opened what is revealed is a nicely shaped female body, the breasts lovely and firm, a fully shaven crotch – and a male penis of no mean proportions. I realise that I have lost the capacity to be shocked for I am scarcely surprised by this vision.

We all repair to a bedroom that reminds me of the more interestingly decorated studies at my public school; the walls are hung with vaguely oriental drapes, the bed is adorned with richly coloured Asian cushions and the whole exotic Eastern effect is enhanced by the smell of joss sticks. In fact, the whole experience is increasingly reminiscent of some surreal English public school fantasy as my friend informs me rather than her – for I gather that he had been before – that he wishes to be buggered.

After taking off my shoes, jacket and tie, I climb onto the king-size double bed and lean with my back against the wall to watch the show. The other two follow. I simply watch as our hostess strips my friend of his garments below the waist while he remains in his shirt and, bizarrely, his tie as he kneels and presents his bottom. Our hostess lubricates himself and then proceeds to effect entry. A number of thrusts later I see my friend grow erect, at which point my mind begins to wander and I am transported back 35 years to my ivy-clad, impeccably British prep school and an early homosexual experience where I was the passive/female party. I suddenly realise what a cliché all my sexual experiences have been.

As my reverie ends I realise I am erect and they have stopped. Indeed, my friend has disappeared to clean himself up. Our hostess looks into my eyes, down to my crotch and then back to my eyes. Nothing is said as he comes over and lies beside me. He undoes my trousers. I slightly lift my hips and my suit trousers and black boxers are pushed down to my knees. As I play with his superb breasts, a credit to the surgeon, without doubt, he plays with me until I come into the baby wipe he has deftly procured from the bedside table.

Afterwards, over a bottle of champagne, I thank my friend for an interesting experience but privately decide that having tried manufactured women twice – and even though I regret nothing – I definitely prefer the real thing.

TEN

'I am about to have sex with a total stranger'

One day, Brad, a longstanding American contact, whose pretty, blonde wife has put on weight and found God in parallel with one another to the horror of my friend, puts it to me that we should spend a night sampling what London has to offer by way of corporate entertainment. He has engaged a chauffeur/guide and wishes me to accompany him. I need little encouragement to accept.

We kick off after a light dinner at around 10 p.m. with a couple of West End clubs. The first is up some stairs in a side street near Piccadilly. Walking through the door requires each of us to pay twenty pounds, though I'm pleased to say both notes come from Brad. Once inside, a number of tired-looking women in tawdry evening dresses sit around in a couple of poorly lit rooms painted mostly black. Indeed, throughout this world I am now sampling, black set off with purple and silver are the predominant colours and all lighting is subdued: much of it strikes me as being like a bad Hammer horror set and I wonder whether the set designers and lighting men moved on to the sex industry when the studios closed down!

At the bar – black again – we are shown the drinks price list. I do not like this at all. The penguin-suited maître d' advises us that the act of sitting with and beginning to converse with one of the establishment's ladies will necessitate the purchase of a bottle of champagne. Despite feeling no desire for any of them whatsoever, out of curiosity I ask a direct question about the possibility of sex, somewhat to Brad's embarrassment. The maître d' is taken aback by my frankness, and indicates that this is not on the agenda, though later I wonder whether he thought we were a couple of plain-clothes policemen trying to entrap him. We leave.

The second venue is in an obscure square. In broad terms, the arrangements are not dissimilar, though the women are younger and more attractive, the lighting better, the maître d' more welcoming and the net effect a lot more enticing.

We are approached by a couple of the ladies and, once I have established that this very act does not require the immediate purchase of a bottle of champagne, sit with them and order a couple of beers. Perhaps the mistake they make is that the one I desire sits with Brad. Or perhaps it is the fact that the purchase of expensive drinks cannot be delayed for long. Either way, I tell Brad we are leaving and, after downing the beers and having thanked the ladies for their company, that is what we do.

We decide that both are expensive rip-off joints frequented by sad, lonely businessmen with over-large expense accounts, little sense and even less courage to go to a straightforward lap-dancing joint like Kaleidoscope. It may be that if you are wealthy enough, it doesn't matter that you spend over £100 on a bottle of very indifferent champagne in order to converse with young women, but it isn't a game either of us is interested in playing. I do not know to this day whether sex would have been an option later in the night but if so, it is an extremely expensive way of paying for it.

Having left both places quickly, I tell our chauffeur/guide that I am entirely underwhelmed by what he has shown us so far.

There follow brief stays at China Whites and the Funky Buddha, conventional West End disco nightclubs frequented by the rich and famous: places where a minor royal might rub shoulders with footballers, tabloid journalists and pop stars. I'm glad I've been once, but do not wish to go again: they make me feel too old, too educated and too poor, in short, like some kind of ageing saddo trying to live a youth he hasn't had.

The evening is not going well and Brad seems to be enjoying it little more than me. The driver now takes us towards London's world-famous Carnaby Street, near which is the Leonora Club.

Some places just get things right and, though expensive, the Leonora is one of them. It's a membership club and our guide has to get us in. From the door, we enter a lobby in which plush carpets, flock wallpaper and brocade curtains are all black trimmed with gold. At the counter is a large man with one of the most welcoming smiles I have ever come across.

'Good evening gentlemen, I gather you wish to take a look at the establishment. Strictly speaking, we are a members-only club and I can't let you in, but as you have been spoken for and clearly look like gentlemen, I think we might allow you. If you would care to drop off your cases, I will escort you downstairs.'

At the bottom, he hands us into the custody of a portly, middle-aged man whose grey hair, plump, knowing face and air of discreet intimacy mark him out as one of life's natural fixers; a man who could arrange anything for you, provided you can and do pay the agreed price. We are introduced to the club.

If fitness for purpose is the hallmark of good design, the Leonora is unsurpassed. Large rooms have been carefully subdivided into separate areas, each of which seamlessly blends into the next to facilitate the way it operates. Unity is further provided by the dark wood and black velvet décor which gives it all an air of opulence.

By the entrance is the bar area, shrouded in semidarkness. It takes a moment or two for the eyes to adjust but there we see a herd of girls sitting gossiping amongst themselves. Customers pass through, as Brad and I do whilst eyeing up what is available – but also we ourselves are being assessed for, in places like this, choice is mutual: both parties have the right to indicate that the other does not meet required standards, whatever these may be.

Beyond the bar, the seating subtly changes from sofa-style to small round tables with the seats built to follow the curve in a manner which positively enforces intimacy. Here Brad and I sit with the 'fixer' as he begins to outline the etiquette of the house. Truth be told, concentration is difficult, for this seating gives way to more open floor, at the end of which is a low stage where the inevitable gyrating dancer is slowly and eye-catchingly shedding her clothes. I drag my attention back to our man as he explains the rules.

'You come in, sit down and have a drink, what would you like?'

Two beers are procured from a hovering waitress dressed in very little.

'No girl approaches you. If you like, you can just sit here and watch the floor show. But if one takes your fancy, you let one of us know and we will arrange for her to join you. You chat for five or ten minutes. If then you like one another, you buy a bottle of champagne for you both to drink. Here is the list. The house champagne is ninety pounds per bottle. You stay talking as long as you like and that may be all you do. But if you want to you can arrange to have sex, not on the premises because that would mean we break the law, but we can arrange a room for you at a number of nearby hotels. The arrangement is between you and the girl but I advise them to charge you at least three hundred pounds, but for that they are expected to stay a good time. So, enjoy yourselves and let me know if there is anyone you want.'

'I like that,' I say to Brad. 'Nice and clear, you know what's what. And I like him and the place and . . . I really rather like *her*,' indicating with a slight turn of the head a slim brunette sitting nearby.

He suggests we get her over and I indicate to a waitress, who duly summons the fixer. Within five minutes, the brunette is sitting between us. She tells us her name is Katherine but to call her Kate and that she is a language student. Brad replies with the self-justificatory line that he's been giving since the beginning of the evening:

'We're a couple of businessmen who are trying to find the right place to entertain some clients.'

There are perhaps a few shreds of truth in this but it largely performs the function of alleviating Brad's self-inflicted guilt at what we are doing. I have no problem with his suggestion, and have already given my wife an honest explanation of what is going on. Brad, by contrast, has informed me that he would be *killed* if his fundamentalist wife knew, and this is his somewhat flimsy explanation to her; though I suspect that in reality she has few illusions. I also think it is of no interest to Kate, who is more concerned about whether she is going to get propositioned, if so by whom, or are we going to suggest a threesome?

She can be no clearer about what we want when, a few minutes later, Brad procures a bottle of champagne, or even half an hour later for by this time Brad and I are beginning to argue. The substance of this becomes clear when Kate goes to the loo.

'I want to have her,' I say.

'But what about me?'

'You choose another one.'

'I can't do that.'

'Why not, there must be somebody else you find attractive and, besides, I saw her first, she's here with us because of me.'

'No, you don't understand,' he says. 'I'm not going to have anyone, I . . . I can't, I don't want to.'

'This is silly. This evening's all about sex, that's why we are here. Now you're telling me when we get to the crunch that you're not going to do it. Why are we doing all this, then?'

'I . . . I . . . the point is, I don't know. I'm just not going to. I might catch something or –'

'Rubbish,' I interrupt. 'In my experience – or more importantly that of one or two of my friends who are more experienced than me – call girls, at least the ones at this level, are the cleanest, most hygiene-conscious people you'll find. If they catch something, their income disappears. You're far more likely to catch something off a casual pick-up, a one-night stand. Someone like Kate really can't afford to catch something because it damages her stock in trade. Get real, Brad, you're being naïve!'

'No, I just don't want to.'

'Well, I do. That's why we're here and if you don't want to, you'll just have to wait for me whilst I do!'

'You'll be two or three hours.'

'I can shorten it.'

'No. It's too long!'

'Sorry, Brad,' I insist. 'I need sex.'

'Well, we'll talk to our driver but I'm not waiting that long.'

I think Kate is genuinely disappointed when we leave shortly thereafter, though that is probably more about the loss of income than about desire for me.

However, as we leave, I join. Formalities completed and fees paid, the resulting membership card will be used regularly by me over the months that follow.

Outside our chauffeur does, indeed, know the where-abouts of a brothel to which he now drives us.

It may be to do with the property market that basements seem to feature so largely in the sex industry, at least in London. Presumably they are less popular for other uses and are therefore available for lower rents. Either way, it somehow seems inevitable that, after I have stopped off at a nearby cash machine, we are taken to a Mayfair address and invited to make our way down some exterior stairs to the basement apartment of an impressive Regency house.

There we are met by the madam, a coarse-looking woman of uncertain age which I would put at about fifty, though this may simply reflect the privations of a relatively hard life – for as I am later to discover, most such madams have been on the game themselves. Becoming a madam is simply the equivalent of the move into management that tends to characterise most professions as the practitioner gets on in years. At the time, my immediate feeling is one of dislike, made all the more so by what is to follow, though arguably she was just doing her job with reasonable efficiency.

The brothel itself is visually unremarkable. Walls are white and the furniture nondescript, though all with that same clichéd, rather subdued lighting.

'Good evening, gentlemen,' she says. 'We have a selection of five ladies for you to choose from tonight.'

Brad is, I suspect, even more nervous than me and very anxious to ensure his part in the proceedings is properly understood.

'I'm just here because he is. I'm just going to sit and wait if that's all right.'

'You'd better just stay and sit here,' she says, motioning him to a chair with a certain irritation because half her income from the two of us has just disappeared.

She then briefly goes away whilst I stand wondering what in hell I am doing. Do we just get down to it? How long have I paid for? Do we have time to chat? What if I don't like any of them? The truth is I am nervous without Harry's smooth direction of events.

I am about to have sex with a total stranger – for the first time on my own initiative.

As I reflect on this, I am brought back to reality by the appearance of five women in their underwear. They stand in a line whilst I am invited to make the judgement of Paris. Most potential tastes are catered for in terms of weight, colouring and ethnicity. I opt for a petite, slim, olive-complexioned brunette, rather ungallantly expressing my wishes by pointing and uttering a monosyllabic 'her'.

The others troop off.

The madam comes close to me. 'A hundred and fifty.'

I pay without comment, after which the girl and I are ushered into a bedroom. As the madam shuts the door, the girl turns and smiles at me, an action which effectively brings Freddy's training on etiquette into play.

I grin back.

'Hello, you're pretty, what's your name and where are you from?'

'I Claudia an' I from Brazil. What you name?'

I tell her.

'You nice man. You have sex with me.'

'Yes, in a minute, but tell me a bit about yourself first.'

We sit on the bed, take one another's hands and look into one another's eyes.

'I Brazilian, I over here six months and I try to save money because back home I wanna be doctor so I can help people.'

'You're really sweet.'

At that moment, I feel for the first time a flood of emotions and thoughts that have recurred regularly since. They reflect my youth. For, like most of my contemporaries first at my public school and then at Oxford, I spent lots of time and money failing to have sex. At that moment, I cannot believe that that is exactly what I am about to enjoy with this sweet, pretty, adorable creature. It is all so easy. I feel towards her a sense of warmth, a rush of affection. I also feel briefly frustrated – frustrated about institutions and social attitudes which during my teens and into my twenties meant that it would have felt shameful to have these experiences when I was at my most potent. Or perhaps I've just grown into a dirty old man!

Throughout my story, these feelings will recur. I love having sex. It is a pinnacle of pleasure, a high I can get no other way. And paying in the way I have has allowed me to reach it with a frequency and a variety I have wanted all my life. I resent the values, the laws, the morality that have quite needlessly made a mountain out of a molehill for so long. For Christ's sake, it's just sex, after all. Why so much unnecessary secrecy and shame?

Claudia does not disappoint. After undressing one another, we lie on the bed side by side just looking at one another, making eye contact. I put my hand out and begin to caress her, stroking her arms, thighs and belly, marvelling at the smoothness of her skin. She responds in kind. Only after a while do I begin to touch her breasts, stroking and gently kneading them before putting my mouth to her nipples, first one then the other. Only after her hand has begun to stroke my now growing erection do I allow my own to begin to explore her sex. I seek to arouse her in the way I do my wife, making circling motions on her thighs and lower belly for some while before seeking out her vaginal lips and clitoris. The fact that I am paying does not mean I do not want to arouse this woman as much as I can, to give her as much pleasure as I can, to make her share my pleasure at the experience she is giving me. Of course, I cannot know the extent to which her response is real or feigned; she is just doing her job. Why it's important to me to please a woman who is being paid to have sex with me I don't know. Perhaps to assuage my guilt or justify my actions.

Once our hands have made us ready, she leans across to find a condom, which she places over me before I enter her. We find a rhythm.

After I come, she takes off the condom and cleans me up.

I tell her, 'You're wonderful, absolutely and completely wonderful.'

She says nothing but smiles in response.

After we've dressed, we exchange kisses on the cheeks.

'Good luck, and I hope the doctoring works out for you.'

In reality I am sceptical about how much of the £150 will make its way to her.

No words are exchanged between Brad and me when I come out or at first in the taxi. Then he can contain himself no longer.

'So, how was it?'

'Fantastic, absolutely bloody fucking fantastic, completely wonderful!'

ELEVEN

'I am now being violated, abused and used for pleasure'

Portcullis House contains one of the nicest and best-value restaurants in London. Generally, its use is confined to MPs, but their research assistants can book it when Members are likely to be in the constituency.

I often go there at Friday lunch time. Generally I much prefer talking to research assistants: they are usually young, attractive, intelligent and, more often than not, female. I can achieve more. They are more appreciative of the hospitality. And I know that what is arranged will actually happen, for a typical researcher is more a person of his or her word than any MP, at least in my experience.

Thus it is that one Friday in late spring, I am sitting down to lunch with a researcher. The menu is mildly adventurous, featuring dishes including anchovies, capers, lemon and ginger jus, raspberry coulis . . .

Lunching with this researcher is a joy, for she is in her early twenties with a Masters degree in economics, and has a good mind, a ready smile and is rather pretty: life sometimes can really be very good.

We are discussing the next steps in my campaign. I have drafted a brief for her to turn into a letter that her MP boss will sign. It happens all the time in politics. People like me are the source of much of the material which ostensibly goes out in the name of your MP.

But my mind is also on matters other than politics. Let me be frank. It will already be clear that I fancy the researcher and there is a frisson of flirtatiousness about the whole conversation. For the subtext underlying the discussion is about giving and receiving, what we can do for one another. I would not actually proposition her – that would be both unprofessional and risk damaging other objectives – but I can fantasise and do so safe in the knowledge that my desires might soon be satisfied.

I am wondering how the research assistant will compare with my next appointment. This is with someone I have never met. All I really know about her is that she is Czech and she works in Harrow.

I found her in the classified column of a local freesheet in a small ad that simply said 'Czech girl' and listed a phone number. This I have rung the day before and after a brief conversation I am due in a flat at 4.30 p.m. I should just have time to get from Westminster to Harrow. It was for all the world like booking an appointment with a hairdresser or any other personal service. It is the beginning of my obsession with Eastern Europe.

I am, of course, nervous but also excited and turned on as much by the switch of location, of woman, of role, as by the sex I know I am going to have. When it is over I will travel back home, have a gin and tonic or some more wine and H will inquire whether I have had a good day, to which I will casually answer, 'Oh, not at all bad!'

It all works exactly as I plan. I even indulge myself in a brandy with the coffee, for the Portcullis restaurant prices are low and my client is paying. Of course, I offer my companion one but I know she will decline as she still has work to do.

When it is time to part, I kiss her chastely enough but nonetheless enjoy the brief moment of physical intimacy.

As the Tube takes me towards Harrow-on-the-Hill, I intermittently muse and read. I always carry a book with me and whether waiting in the central lobby of the House, travelling on the Tube or at a loose end in a bar, I fill idle minutes with this. The relevance of this to my story is that over the months I have read a lot of evolutionary biology. The nature of man as they set it out, the sexual strategies, the desires and duplicity of the clever ape, all provide a backdrop of self-justification. I use it as a conversational gambit in business and in my pleasure. At that moment I am starting down this road with Jared Diamond's *Why is Sex Fun?*, a totally serious book.

Leaving the station, I ring my anonymous Czech so she can talk me through the short walk that takes me to an entirely undistinguished but perfectly pleasant three-storey apartment building. I ring the intercom bell and am told to go to the nearest ground-floor flat. Working girls and their maids have a characteristic way of opening doors. They make use of spyholes, door chains and all the paraphernalia designed to allay their fears, for they can have no more idea of how I will behave and whether I will cause problems than I do of whether their appearance and sexuality will satisfy me. But for them, unlike for me, the unknown is a source of trepidation rather than anticipation. So the door is opened only a few inches, and a blonde mane and blue eyes peer around it before she decides that I look acceptable and am ushered in.

She takes me straight to the bedroom, which has a bed, a chair and no decoration. We appraise one another. She is slightly taller than me in her heels, but will become shorter without them, is curvy without being fat and has the wide-open face of many Slavs.

Guessing that she initially wants reassurance that I will be no trouble, I immediately go to my wallet and pay the £120 we have agreed. It would be difficult to decide which of the two of us is the more nervous as we smile at one another for the first time, sit on the bed and begin to talk, exchanging names and key details. She tells me, and I believe her, that she is a student, has only been here for three months and has only been doing this for a couple of weeks. She says that the ad was the first she has run and I am only her third customer, with an innocence and newness which I appreciate because it is like my own.

Then she says, 'I mad, crazy girl to be doing this.'

'Why, what makes you think that?'

'I bad girl. I should not do it. I not tell my mother or boyfriend.'

'I'm sure you're not bad, for how else can a student, especially a foreign one, better earn money? What you are doing is the rational response of an attractive young woman to economic necessity. There's a traditional phrase in English. What you are doing is described as the oldest profession in the world. This happens the world over and there is nothing wrong with it. Besides, you're very pretty.'

I don't know how much of this she understands but I have to try. For, at that moment, building her self-esteem and justifying what she is doing is vital to my own sense of self-worth and the belief that I am not in my turn behaving unreasonably.

As we talk, we have begun to undress, me to nakedness, her to a pair of lacy red knickers. Words are replaced by action as we fall silent, lie back on the bed and begin to caress one another.

'Will you roll over?' I ask.

'Why you want this?'

I think she fears I am about to assault her in some way.

'I want to see and fondle your bottom.'

Hesitantly she does as I ask. I caress her bottom then lean across and kiss it, running my finger down the line of its crack.

She stops this by rolling over and, with us now facing one another once again, she kisses my lips, then my chest. My excitement now clear, concentration switches to the genitals, progressing inexorably to the inevitable conclusion. She is more passive than the Brazilian.

Afterwards, as I relax for a few minutes, then dress, I am filled with elation, a feeling that sustains me on the journey home and through my conversation with H, over a gin and tonic, about our respective days. I tell her no lies but merely omit what has been the high point of my week. Yet I never go back or ring the Czech again for I am certain that other, better opportunities await.

Two and a half weeks pass and it is time for a quarterly review meeting. I take a taxi to a modernised Edwardian building on the edge of the City. It is a place of transition where the refurbished elegance and towers of the banks and financial institutions begin to give way to older, meaner buildings which soon run into the combination of Bohemianism, poverty and squalor of Hoxton and Hackney.

The area seems an appropriate metaphor for how I am now living.

Once there, I give a PowerPoint® presentation running through what we are doing and why. The combination of Parliamentary questions, meetings with MPs and ministers, and the 150 signatures on the Early Day Motion demonstrates that we are making progress. But our goal – the jewel in the crown – is the Office of Fair Trading. It and its dry economic logic is what matters, not the pomposities of Westminster and the empty rhetoric of its inhabitants.

In the dull moments, I reflect on how my whole life seems to be an interesting commentary on whether or not perception is reality. I finish the presentation and the meeting lasts another couple of hours before I go back to join them for a late lunch. I am feeling pleased with myself, and on the spur of the moment, as I pass a phone box, I go inside.

I am soon having the following conversation.

'I'm ringing about your ad.'

'Where are you ringing from?'

I give her my location.

'We're not far away. We have two girls for you to choose from today. A five-foot-nine, size-ten blonde and a five-foot-six, size-twelve brunette, both very pretty.'

'How much?'

'It starts at forty pounds for hand relief.'

'The address?'

I have soon walked the short distance to the place she has named, in a short alley off a side street in Clerkenwell. It is a set of flats half-hidden amidst a jumble of modernised Victorian and Edwardian buildings and 1960s and 70s construction. The flat itself is nice and airy.

The tough-looking maid plants me in a bedroom and then brings in two girls dressed in negligees and looking exactly as described, except that the blonde is quite simply one of the most beautiful women I have ever seen. The choice is no contest and I pay the maid £80 for half an hour with the blonde.

I do not know it at the time (due to my inexperience) but have learned since that a sure sign that a working girl is a free agent is that you negotiate and pay her directly.

The maid returns with the blonde, who comes into the room hesitantly. I try to begin a conversation.

'Hi! Where are you from?'

'Norwegian.'

'So how long have you been over here?'

'You want sex?' she asks.

'Yes, but let's talk first. I want to know about you.'

'We have sex.'

Conversation stops as she gets on the bed. I undress, join her and try again to have a conversation.

'You're beautiful, you know, quite stunning. In fact, one of the best-looking women I have ever met.'

She does not answer and half-heartedly pushes away my hands as I begin to try to stroke her.

I persist. 'Isn't it nicer to get to know one another first?'

My final attempt to talk is equally unsuccessful, so she is entirely silent and largely passive as I fondle her very lovely body.

As soon as she judges I am ready, she pulls away to get a condom, rolls it on and impales herself upon me. Doing all the work, her movement is vigorous but reflects only a desire to get it over with, not any enthusiasm for the activity.

Afterwards I say 'thank you' but she never utters another word as she wipes herself and goes out, leaving me to recover and dress.

As I stroll back, I reflect on the fact that she manifestly did not want to have sex with me.

It prompts my next step a few days later.

Contemplating my behaviour with the 'Norwegian', the fact that she really did not want sex and the hidden pressures which might have made her do it, I feel guilty. Should I have saved her? I know what I have to do. Whether it is a conscious choice or whether I am driven by something inside me that is nonetheless beyond my control is irrelevant to the facts of my actions.

I find an ad. It shows a good-looking blonde. I phone the number and within an hour am ringing the doorbell of an upmarket flat close to the Piccadilly Line.

The blonde is all that I hope for. Golden hair cut in a bob frames immaculate make-up straight out of 1940s Hollywood, with scarlet lips and eyes heavy with mascara. A figure-hugging, off-the-shoulder dress both covers and reveals seductive curves.

My extreme anxiety must be readily apparent for my arm is gently taken and a 'don't worry' is whispered breathily in my ear as I am led into a sitting room decked out with impeccable and expensive taste; everything about the place screams class.

I pick Earl Grey from an offer of several teas and watch as, with sinuous movements, my hostess retreats into the kitchen.

On her return, I am asked to tell her about myself which I do, confessing my political involvement whilst worrying that with every word I am putting myself at risk of public exposure and humiliation for no good reason whatsoever. Perhaps, in this case, the confession is at some subconscious level an essential part of the self-abasement.

My tea finished, my hand is taken once again and I am led through to a bedroom whose opulence matches everything else. Burgundy trimmed with gold are the predominant colours of the carefully matched decoration and bedding. I know that I have found the exact requirement for the insane fantasy I am in the grip of.

Up to this point, we have both behaved like two friends of friends meeting for tea. There has been no discussion of anything to do with sex, let alone money.

She explains, 'I get to know the person first and decide what I want to charge. Time is not important. You will stay as long as I want you to. For you, it will be three hundred pounds – that's amongst my lowest rates, by the way, so you may consider yourself flattered!'

I pay without comment.

Her undressing of me begins with little comments on my appearance.

'Hmm, tie from Liberty, good boy, and a proper Jermyn Street double-cuffed shirt, but your cuff links are cheap tat and your shoes are dirty.'

Once I am naked, I am gently pushed down onto the bed.

Turning away, she makes a performance of slipping off her own dress, unveiling her body like the work of art it is. The breasts are improbably magnificent, more surgeon's art, the skin smooth and blemish-free.

After climbing onto the bed, she lies on top of me and turns a kiss into an act of physical assault, thrusting her tongue into my mouth and then withdrawing it only to thrust again. I know I am being orally violated and I simply let it happen, for this time, I have no will of my own in anything. I let my body relax into whatever she is doing to me, for this is just the beginning.

I am stroked and pinched, her hands roaming over my anatomy. She particularly likes what I think of as the crevasses, so she occupies my armpits and gropes the places where my legs meet my torso before rolling me over and running two fingers along the crease of my bum several times.

I think of nothing and simply let all this happen, aware only of the physical sensations, which are pleasurable but edged with roughness and pain.

Abruptly stopping, she pulls me up. Pillows are adjusted and she now lies back but against the bedhead so she is more sitting up than lying down, a position from which she can continue to exercise control, which she does by guiding my head down to her crotch where I am expected to lick her rampant shaft.

'Take the entire head in.'

I do as I am told and feel her filling my mouth. It is the first penis I have ever had in my mouth, and is an experience I know I will never repeat.

'Keep in as much as you can but concentrate on using your tongue on the underside where the head meets the shaft.'

As I obey her orders, her hands resume their invasion of my bottom, gripping and kneading my buttocks, stroking again along the crease before I feel a finger pressing insistently on the dimple of my anus.

She leans over, decants some of the lubricant conveniently placed on the bedside table and, as I continue to suck, her finger penetrates me.

'Time to fuck you!'

As she acquires a condom, I assume the classic position of submission, kneeling with my bottom in the air and my face buried in the bed, the kowtow of the Chinese imperial court. I am completely open and exposed to her ravages as she anoints my anus with large quantities of oil, grips my thighs and begins to penetrate me.

'You're a virgin, aren't you? I knew that the moment you walked in the door. Relax, don't fight it and it won't hurt too much.'

I carry on doing as I am told. I think of what? Nothing at first, and then an image of a medieval monarch's bedchamber. I imagine I am a fifteen-year-old peasant totally unused to the luxury that comes as a by-product of the fact that I am now being violated, abused and used for pleasure. And I know that this is why I have come, for it is what I deserve.

Again, my mind empties simply to experience the sensation of being occupied without say or will or any control whatsoever over my own destiny.

My mind oscillates between emptiness (except sensation), and images from history: of battlefields, prisons, smoking ruined villages, the torture chamber of the Inquisition, shackles, racks, American black slaves, white Roman slaves, for this is what man does to man, though more often man is doing it to woman.

And I know that as a politician, this is what I am involved in, the endless round of inflicting on people a suffering they do not deserve and I know that however clever I am, however much I anticipate the unintended consequence, this is what I am likely to do, for politics is about using force to compel people to do what they would not do left to themselves.

She ends my reverie by telling me that she has come. I slump down on the bed and lie there doing nothing while she cleans herself and then me. Still I do nothing as she begins to massage my body, but this is no pre-sexual teasing, it is the real McCoy as she expertly manipulates every inch of my body from head to toe. She does briefly play with my manhood but it is totally unresponsive.

As I dress, she lies watching me.

'Don't worry, I get myself checked every three months, everything we did was perfectly safe. You will find yourself feeling weak and shaky, that's perfectly normal. Thank you for giving me your virginity, it's always a pleasure to take someone's.'

As she sees me out, she adds, 'Next time, clean your shoes, don't wear anything cheap and bring me chocolates, champagne and flowers as well.'

I know there will be no next time but I am still grateful for the experience and particularly for the warning about the lassitude. It does not kick in until the following morning but when I wake, thank God it is a Saturday for I can scarcely walk when I first get up.

However, the evening itself is not yet finished. On the off chance I ring a London councillor I know. He is not from my party but still a good friend for, as any politician will tell you, one's friends are not necessarily on one's own side, nor are one's enemies from the other.

As I hope, he is able to meet up and half an hour later we are sitting opposite one another with a bottle of Pinot Grigio between us.

He tells me of the doings of a gay colleague. The man is clever, highly educated and aspires to the highest office. Nonetheless, quite regularly, the colleague puts anything breakable out of reach, drapes dustsheets over the better items of furniture and spreads a large rubber sheet over the floor of his elegant London flat.

He then invites over certain friends and they play a wrestling game. The film *Fight Club* captures the atmosphere. Bruising is suffered and skin broken. The victor 'uses' the defeated.

Have I assuaged my guilt? In the days that follow, I know that I should have behaved differently. I try to go back to the Norwegian's place of business but it has disappeared. What I do know is that what I did was not honourable and I know this sounds ludicrously naïve for one cannot 'save' a prostitute, but I am plagued by thoughts that I should have offered her a means of escape. Given the chance again, I would and I still wish I could and had.

TWELVE

'I like your face and know you will be gentle'

I am a member of a couple of government quangos, the advisory bodies which help shape government policy. The posts are unpaid but carry influence and put me in the most minor of ways amongst those often described as 'the great and the good'. We regularly meet ministers to discuss policy, though I wonder how useful it is, for most politicians only hear what they want to hear. Most of the time, their minds are closed.

As I leave one of these meetings in Victoria, my mobile rings. It is Harry. At first we discuss business, but then the conversation moves on. He has a suggestion in which I might be interested.

Ten days later, we meet at his office to travel together to one of the expensive hotels on the north side of the Bath Road near Heathrow. He has told me to bring at least £300.

He does not have a room number but has to make a call when we arrive at an expensive and extensive hotel suite: there are two good-sized double bedrooms, with a sitting room between and both a kitchen and bathroom off the small entrance lobby.

At the door is a tall, handsome mixed-race woman, dressed in figure-hugging leopard print.

'Hi, guys, good to see you, glad that you could make it. Neither of you have been before, have you?'

Harry says not.

'Well, first can you put the cash in one of these envelopes and put your name on it so that that's taken care of? And I suggest you put all valuables, wallets, mobiles and so on in this second envelope, which you also give to me with your name on it so you know nothing important will go missing. Then if you undress in the bathroom, putting your clothes in one of the wardrobes and putting on one of the towelling robes, then come back to the sitting room and have a glass of champagne.'

This we do while taking in the sight of the other men – at least a dozen of them. None of us can be under thirty or over fifty. Each of us gives every impression by accent, by appearance and by style of being reasonably well heeled and middle class. The clothing – seen in the wardrobes rather than being worn by their owners – is all business suits, jackets, ties, real leather shoes and briefcases.

The women, of whom there are five, are all young, attractive according to taste, and wearing baby-dolls or lingerie. They seem rather more at ease than the men as we chat, smile and drink, for all the world like a cocktail party conducted in dressing gowns and sexy underwear. I learn that one comes from Bournemouth and is a student and two others are from Nottingham, where they seem to be professional call girls.

When she judges everybody ready, our hostess addresses the girls and tells them to begin. The girls invite us to join them in the bedrooms, each of them taking two or three of us. For no particular reason I go with a brunette and two blokes, whilst Harry goes with someone else. Once in the bedroom, the brunette is soon playing with two men, one of which is me, whilst being groped by three. English good manners come into play and I and one of the others give way to the most aroused amongst us. The brunette is nothing if not game, however, and is prepared to carry on using her hands and be fondled even as she gives head.

We are, of course, not alone, as the emperor-sized bed is also occupied by one of the other girls and a couple of her admirers.

Having used her mouth to good effect on man one, I watch as my companion takes her in the missionary position. When he is finished, she looks at me, smiles, and says, 'Your turn next, but first I must go the bathroom.'

And, indeed, I now notice that she is visibly perspiring from her efforts.

When she returns, I am lying on the bed so she straddles me, puts my hands on her breasts and rides me until I come. Next to us, a blonde is having another man.

Satisfied, I wander back into the sitting room for further champagne and a couple of the sandwiches on offer. Our hostess asks if I am enjoying myself and I agree that I am.

Even as we talk another girl comes up to me and invites me to join her. This time we go into the other room where I see Harry in action. We share a bed with a couple of women and a couple of blokes.

I am unable to come so soon, but still thoroughly enjoy the action with first one then another of the girls.

Later, Harry and I share a quiet conversation over more champagne.

'Enjoying yourself?' he asks.

'Yes, you?'

'I was but now I'm getting bored.'

'Oh?'

'There are limits to just how many women one wants and, to be honest, though they are nice enough, there's nothing particularly to my taste.'

'You mean there is nobody black?'

'Actually I fancy our hostess but I don't think she is available.'

I smile.

'And that doesn't surprise me because I was wondering whether she's a transsexual – she's certainly masculine enough.'

Our conversation is disturbed by the subject of our conversation announcing the floor show.

At this point a petite blonde, who I have not yet had but have talked to and certainly desire, takes my hand and leads me slightly apart from the others. She explains my role in the forthcoming proceedings, including why she has picked me. 'I like your face and know you will be gentle,' she says, and hands me the necessary equipment.

The show begins with two of the girls stripping and fondling one another. As their caresses grow more impassioned, my diminutive blonde friend appears wearing a leather bridle, through which her long blonde hair is shaped to form a ponytail, and a strap-on dildo. After some initial stroking, she uses the dildo to enter the uppermost of the pair. That is my cue. I move to the animated group, check the equipment she has given me is properly lubricated and then gently caress her bottom until my finger is entering her anus. I then begin to insert the rounded end of the tool. Taking care not to be too vigorous, I push it all the way into her bottom. With that, my role is finished and I retire to watch.

As the other end of the instrument contains a second ponytail not unlike her own, what we see is a lesbian sandwich of which the uppermost girl is attired somewhat like a horse with tails from head and bottom, a spectacle as much comic as erotic with everyone, including the participants, smiling and laughing. Eventually, with much sighing, they come, or at least pretend to.

When it is over, I seek out my little blonde and help remove her harness.

'I didn't hurt you?'

'No, you were great.'

'So were you. You're completely lovely and I want you very much.'

'Give me a few minutes to clean up and we can probably have a bed to ourselves.'

She is right, for when she comes back to me, everybody seems to have had everybody (at least who they want) and one of the bedrooms is now empty. She leads me into it and, though the door is open, we have something not too far off relative privacy. The resulting activity is unhurried – we have both had much sex and I at least want this to be gentle and beautiful for I find her very desirable. Thus it is quite some minutes before I have a second, quite mind-blowing, climax.

Afterwards, I realise that Harry and others have been within earshot at least during the latter stages.

'God, you're a noisy bugger,' he says.

Of the other males in all this, I learn little, though one of the men says at one stage that he is 'something in concrete', to which another says that he is 'in rubber'. He appears not to be aware just how amusing this is.

I enjoyed myself enough to repeat the experience on a second occasion a couple of months later. It is more or less identical to the first, although, rather to my regret, my blonde is not amongst the girls and I am unable to play the role of her 'groom'. This time, I go without Harry, but instead take another friend whom I have thus introduced to Heathrow sex parties.

THIRTEEN

'This kind of behaviour needs to be punished'

After all sensible people have finished their holidays – for the days have begun to grow appreciably shorter and the English weather has acquired its autumnal damp chill – the British political community decamps to the seaside for the annual party conferences.

This year, work commitments take me to all three, the Liberal Democrats in Brighton, Labour in Bournemouth and the Tories in Blackpool.

You could say I go mad.

It is not entirely my own doing, at least to start with, for I have gone to the Liberal Democrats conference almost exclusively to renew contacts with one of their MPs. Before I see him, I am supposed to meet my client at the Old Ship hotel where I have booked us rooms.

I wait at the appointed time, reading *The Times* and then the *Independent*. After twenty minutes, I ring the MP's office to discover that as far as their secretary is aware he and his researcher are meeting me. I try their mobiles.

Switched off. Another fifteen minutes and I leave a message at reception: I am now free and alone. I walk back in the direction of the conference centre wondering who I might bump into, with whom I want to drink and whether I have their mobile number.

I pass a telephone booth. Glancing in is a habit long since acquired in London where there is scarcely a telephone box in much of Westminster which doesn't offer myriad sexual possibilities – provided you have the money.

Brighton has been described as Camden-on-sea and it is presumably entirely appropriate that it should follow London's 'carding' convention. A central London telephone box can have anything over a dozen cards. The degree of sophistication varies from what is no more than a handwritten slip with a few words and a telephone number through to a quality piece of marketing. Many are clear about the specialism on offer: 'Stunning showgirl – over 6ft of goddess' with a Vargas print for those liking more Amazonian women; 'Naughty Kim Needs Strict Correction' with a photo of a busty blonde sitting on a bed; 'Slaves come and serve this merciless mistress' with a silver on black drawing of a corseted, whip-carrying dominatrix; or 'Mistress Maya Mystical Tantric Massage Erotic Tie & Tease with Silks & Pearls Cuffs & Leather Supreme Body Worship . . . This is not a dungeon, 30 something, English, Cultured and Educated, private artistic surroundings' with a black-and-white photograph of a silent movie actress and a long string of pearls.

The two cards that catch my eye in Brighton (multiple copies of each allowing me to take them) offer 'Foxy Ladies . . . After Dark Discreetly situated between the Seafront and Western Road' and 'Night Desires one minute from clock tower'.

Two telephone calls later, I am seeking out a particular entry-phone near the clock tower and twenty minutes after that am having sex with an Australian student who started her professional life in the legalised brothels of Sydney and is working her way around the world. We agree that the Australian system of full legalisation rather than the authorities turning a blind eye but having the excuse to bust anybody they want to is a better way to organise these things. It is, however, not a point I make to the MP I had arranged to meet earlier when I bump into him and his ever delightful and helpful research assistant an hour or so later. We go for a coffee and discuss our campaign for by now he is as committed to reforming what he perceives as injustice as I am.

I drift back to the Old Ship, check for nonexistent messages and fall asleep in my room watching *Neighbours*.

Having sampled 'Night Desires' (albeit in the afternoon) I decide to try 'Foxy Ladies'. The place itself is in a narrow street off the seafront near the conference centre and the Grand Hotel. This means I might be seen by fellow conference-goers who know me. Turning into the road itself, I affect a nonchalant stroll as if to say to any passer-by, 'Hey, I could be in any street in Brighton, I haven't picked this one, honest.' When I see the right number – and most such establishments use large well-lit numbers to aid their customers – I glance round furtively to check there is nobody about before I press the bell. To avoid the unfortunate chance encounter, I want to get inside as quickly as possible. My furtive behaviour feels like something out of a bad movie.

Once inside, I am offered a choice of four girls. I opt for an olive-skinned Brazilian whose English is poor but sexual technique excellent. I am reminded of the lady of Mayfair, but this one seems more in control of her own destiny, the relationship between her and the maid one of equals. This pleases me and helps to contribute to a very satisfactory experience, for with all these women I do not want to think that I am aiding their exploitation. It matters to me that she should be a free agent choosing this way of earning a living rather than somebody exploited, manipulated and abused by a pimp. I cannot ever be certain, but manner, body language, bearing and enthusiasm all contrive to convey whether the particular working girl is working under duress. With the experience of the Norwegian at the back of my mind, I now look for these things.

My exit is as ridiculous as my entrance as I stand at the door, peer out to check the street is empty in both directions and then set off at a brisk pace for the cover of the seafront. Ten minutes later I am in the bar of the Grand Hotel drinking with one of their election candidates. She introduces me to a number of her friends. Thus I pass pleasant hours drinking with idealistic, enthusiastic, motivated, bright young people who are the lifeblood of all future political success, at least in democracies. Without them, a party has no future. By this criterion, the Liberal Democrats most certainly do.

This almost surreal alternation between discussing how to run the country with its current and future leaders, and disappearing for surreptitious sex, characterises all three weeks.

It reaches its zenith the following week in Bournemouth at the conference of the Labour party.

I discover Tanya on my second night, a little way off the beaten track on the Christchurch Road. It is 1 a.m., I am her last customer of the night and I have to wait for her. I am assured it will be well worth it as I chat over a cup of coffee with the maid, a very nice woman younger than many of her kind.

Tanya appears about twenty minutes later. She is a pretty brunette about my height, and I conclude she must be in her late twenties or early thirties. She is dressed in stockings, suspenders, thong and basque, the whole a visual fantasy in black and red.

'Hello, sorry you had to wait. Now what can I do for you?' This is said with a smile and a brightness of manner which puts me completely at ease and excites me at the same time. This woman is electric: sexy, engaging and full of natural charm. I am simply bowled over. We agree on £60 and she leaves the room briefly as they all do to stow the money safely away.

Once I am undressed, she suggests I lie on my stomach.

'Oil or talc?' she asks.

'Whichever you prefer, I leave it to you, you're the expert.'

'Oil, then. It's messier, but I can do more with it.'

She slips off her heels but otherwise remains dressed as she straddles me, pours a little oil on my back and begins to massage it into my neck and shoulders. I am aware of the pressure of her stockinged legs and lacy thong on my lower back and bottom as her hands work their magic.

Slowly she works down my body until she is sitting on my calves and her hands are working on my buttocks.

'Lift yourself a bit.'

I comply and her hands slide under me, beginning to massage my balls and the base of my penis. This continues for what seem long minutes as she teases me to a pitch of arousal.

'Roll over. I need to wipe the oil off because it affects the rubber.'

A wet-wipe and a soft towel prepare me for the condom.

My own hands have meanwhile become active, caressing her thighs and bottom.

With rapid, sinuous grace, she removes her thong and slowly sinks down onto me. She leans forward over me, smiling, and doing all the work but allowing my hands free rein. As I come to a shuddering orgasm, she smiles down at me.

'God, you're good. That was wonderful.'

'Why, thank you, sir.'

'If you don't mind the question, is there anyone lucky enough to be your man?'

'There was, but not now. He didn't think he was so lucky and we split up. I didn't do this then, of course. I only began it because we needed the money, that's me and my teenage son.'

'How on earth could any man not go to the ends of the earth to keep you?'

'Kind of you to say so, but you know the way these things happen. Anyway, what about you? I guess you're married?'

I briefly tell her about H and the boys, then ask, 'Can I see you again tomorrow?'

'Yes, I'm on tomorrow, starting about two.'

I make an assignation for 4 p.m. The brothel employs a driver who will collect me.

Back at my hotel, it is 3 a.m. but my colleagues are still at the bar.

'Where have you been?'

'The local brothel.'

'Don't be silly!'

'Yes, I have.'

'Come on, stop teasing. Who've you been meeting?'

I tell them I've been meeting with a senior figure in the Labour party and tell them something of the conversation which I had indeed had with the person – *before* my encounter with Tanya. As we talk, I reflect on the fact that I have told them the bald truth and they do not believe me. Now I have misled them, they believe I am being truthful. It is not the first time this has happened. I have a Savile Row suit bought in Oxfam. It has provoked admiring comment.

If I say where I actually bought it, I am accused of being a smartarse. Lie and I am believed.

I get up late and do not get to the conference until late morning. Suddenly, I see an MP. I have never spoken to her in my life but recognise her and affect intimacy.

'Hello, how are you? Good to see you again.'

This is technically true. I have seen her before but I know that she has not a clue who I am. However, as a public figure she does not dare risk insulting me by admitting this.

Soon I have drawn her into a small coterie of colleagues and we all act like old mates.

I repeat this performance many times. Some of the MPs I do know quite well but, mostly, I am playing on the vulnerability of politicians to a combination of flattery and the need to be liked by the public. I am, though, working largely on autopilot, my mind like that of a child awaiting a party as I look forward to four o'clock, which cannot come too soon.

After greeting one another like old friends, the occasion begins like its predecessor but only until Tanya removes her thong. This time she reverses herself over me and we adopt the classic '69' position. Mouths, tongues and hands hyperactive, our enthusiasm is boundless and mutual.

As I continue, she begins to writhe, her mouth comes away from me and her breathing is irregular.

'Sorry, I've just become too sensitive. I hope you don't mind but you'll have to stop.'

'Mind? I think you've just paid me one of the greatest compliments I've ever had in my entire life.'

We smile at one another as she moves round and crouches between my legs. I watch her face as her tongue rolls up and down my penis, then my own eyes close, I lie back and I come in the most stupendous orgasm that seems to go on for ever.

This time, after a clean-up, we just lie there facing one another.

'So how do you get on with your son?'

'OK, but he's a prig and a prude. He's the one that tells me off for wearing miniskirts and going out clubbing and coming home late, pissed.'

'How do you react?'

'I tell him to get a life. He's a nerd, at his computer all day. He needs a girlfriend, to get laid.'

'Presumably he doesn't know what you do?'

'Not on your life.'

'So how do you find the job itself?'

'The work's easy, I choose my hours and most of the blokes are OK. Sometimes I meet really interesting ones, like you.'

'And having so much sex?'

'I sometimes get sore, but generally it's all right.'

'You're certainly absolutely bloody wonderful at it,' I tell her.

She laughs. Suddenly conscious of time, I glance at my watch. 'Look, it's long past any time I've paid for but I'm really enjoying –'

'Oh, you don't have to go. You will if another customer comes, mind.'

By now we are slowly and gently fondling one another again. She asks me about myself. Carefully concealing my own identity, I tell her about politics. She's interested in whom I've met and what I think of them.

As we talk, I learn about her decision to do this to meet the mortgage payments when her husband left her. She was briefly on state benefit but it wasn't enough.

I look at my watch and realise that I am very shortly supposed to be in a meeting.

'Christ, I'm going to be late, I've got to go. Is your driver available? And can I come back and see you again later?'

Laughing, she says, 'You're insatiable. I'll get him.'

The speaker at my meeting is a newly appointed minister whose political outlook I do not find sympathetic.

In the brothel's car, I reflect that listening to her is for me a bit like supping with the devil. And I am buoyed up by thinking just how much she would disapprove of my behaviour. This perverse pleasure carries me through during her address and subsequent questions. I take notes and work out how I will incorporate, in the document I am writing for my client, allusions and references to her thinking which will predispose her to be sympathetic when a copy lands on her desk.

Three glasses of wine later it has finished and I am back with the gorgeous Tanya. The sex is more languid and affectionate than last time, at least that is how I feel about it. We talk: I am telling her about my previous meeting and my feelings about it as I raise my thighs and she caresses me, a combination I find so piquant that I am practically coming. Fortunately in this context, my age is of benefit for I do not yet do so. There is time for us to readopt the '69' position and then, at her suggestion, she kneels on the bed and I take her from behind, my hands cupping her breasts.

To, I think, our mutual disappointment, this time there is another customer so it has to end.

As I dress, I say, 'I have only one regret.'

She looks surprised and concerned.

'It's that I live and work in London, so seeing you again will be difficult if not impossible and you are quite literally amongst the best experiences of my entire life – you're just wonderful.'

'I wondered for a moment what you were going to say then,' she replies. 'I wondered what I could possibly have got wrong, but that's OK. You're pretty special yourself, so do come and see me if you are down this way.'

As I leave, I buy from her a memento, the freshly published edition of *McCoys*. This is a comprehensive guide to the UK sex industry available on the web and in book form. It provides a county-by-county guide to massage parlours, escort agencies and sole practitioners, giving not only listings and contact details but also star ratings.

If the police were actually interested in stopping prostitution, it and the web provide a definitive list of those to target. Thankfully, they are not. Tanya shows me with pride her description: '. . . in Tanya, a brunette in her thirties, they have a regular superstar. Very amenable to reasonable suggestions and great fun in the room, be prepared for a whale of a time with this lass.'

As I leave Bournemouth the next morning, I can only concur.

By the time of the Tory conference the following week, I am increasingly tired and jaded.

Nonetheless I decide to explore the possibilities and turn to the copy of *McCoys* I bought from Tanya. I make my way to a three-star local brothel. Perhaps I am tired, but it is all dreary and depressing: the woman is English, working class, bored and not in the first flush of youth. I make my apologies – 'Sorry, not my type' – and leave.

The conference does, however, serve its purpose in business terms and I emerge well equipped to help the education charity I am now advising. As a result, a month or so later I have knocked out the first draft of a major policy statement. I am particularly pleased with it, as I have managed to set their thinking in a historical context, highlighting the sheer physical unpleasantness and brutality of education for most children before the 1960s.

> Every now and again, Mr Harby would swoop down to examine exercise books ... Many children he sent out to the front with these books. And after he had thoroughly gone through the silent and quivering class he caned the worst offenders well, in front of the others, thundering in real passion of anger and chagrin.
>
> *The Rainbow* – DH Lawrence

This is playing in my mind as I leave their London offices: I pass a number of phone boxes, all with cards. One offers 'submissive services' and I take a spur of the moment decision to imitate Mr Harby's role. This choice perfectly illustrates how one's spontaneous impulses actually come from subconscious thought, for though the decision is impulsive, doing this has been on my mind as a result of my work for some months now.

A phone call later, I walk to a flat in Earl's Court, inevitably and appropriately, the basement of a five-storey Victorian or Edwardian house, not far from the Tube station. Because this will be a new experience and I am not at all sure I entirely approve of what I am doing, I am nervous as I make my way down the steps adjacent to the rather grander ones that lead to the main front door.

I am let in by a curvy young woman who, although I am sure is in her twenties, has soft, almost childlike features and a pleasingly youthful appearance. She is wearing a white shirt and miniskirt. It will take only a moment to turn her appearance into that of a sexy schoolgirl. We say hello and she leads me through to a room with a bed and an old-fashioned school desk in it as well as a couple of chairs and a wardrobe. The walls are hung with outfits in various sizes to allow almost any fantasy: doctors, nurses, waitresses, teachers with gown and mortar board, baby-dolls, corsets ... The shoe and boot collection is equally impressive and multi-sized to cater for the male customer who wants to take on any of these roles.

'You rang five minutes ago?'

'Yes.'

'So you want me to be submissive?'

'Yes.'

'Do you simply want to use your hand or a cane?'

'What's the cost and how does it work?' I ask.

'Right, I'll dress up in any outfit you like and you can smack me as much as you want to, though you must stop immediately if I tell you to and have sex with me, all for eighty pounds. Use of the cane is extra at ten pounds a stroke.'

'I think the hand will do and, sorry to be so clichéd, but, as you're young and pretty, I'm afraid it's the schoolgirl thing.'

'Stockings or socks?'

'Stockings,' I say, paying her.

'Do you want a bit of role-play?'

'Yes, if that's OK?'

'Most customers do. Shall I seduce you and then you can spank me for doing it before yielding? That usually goes down pretty well.'

'Sounds perfect.'

She disappears through an open door screened by bamboo strings and reappears five minutes later, having added a tie, boater and blazer to her outfit.

'Hello, sir, how are you today?'

'I'm fine, thank you, young lady. Aren't you supposed to be in class?'

'Well, sir, I decided that class is boring and I'd much rather see you, sir, because you're sexy, very sexy.'

By now she is in front of me, running her tongue over her lips, putting a hand on my chest.

'That's no way to behave.'

'Isn't it, sir? Because I think you like it, in fact I can tell that you like it.'

Her other hand begins to explore my crotch.

'This kind of behaviour needs to be punished.'

'Oh, sir, you wouldn't, would you?'

'You, young lady, are going to get what you deserve.'

I take her arm and lead her to the desk. I take my jacket off and put it on a chair. She takes off my tie whilst I sit back on the desk. I pull her towards me and, as she has no bra, fondle her small breasts through the thin material of her shirt.

'Ooh, sir, you shouldn't do that.'

'I'll show you what I should do.'

With that I pull her across my lap. Her boater falls off. I raise her skirt and caress her bottom, at first through the knickers and then naked flesh after I have pulled them down to her knees. My hand parts her legs and I feel that she is clean-shaven.

After much fondling and having gently pinched her buttocks a couple of times, I begin to smack her with my right hand, gently at first because I do not actually want to hurt this woman who I rather like but, when there is no protest, somewhat harder.

As I smack her, I am again eleven and it is me who is going to be beaten and the agent of my punishment is the woman I wish to marry.

She was a teacher at my prep school, about five-foot-seven with light-brown hair, blue eyes and delicate features in a face that was refined and ladylike in repose but which came alive when animated by a smile. Her body was slim but above all beautifully proportioned. Her hair was long, although she usually wore it up during the day, as she judged this appropriate to the classroom. But the most striking aspect was her dress sense, which much of the time would not have disgraced a Mayfair cocktail party. She wore business suits with silk blouses and flowery dresses, all of which had the short miniskirt of the age, showing off her smooth, shapely legs to perfection.

I was smitten, gazing at her and being there as much as possible if she needed a pupil to run any small errands.

It is perhaps ironic that it was she who was responsible for the sole occasion in my entire school career that I was beaten. My crime was to be out of bed after lights out on the penultimate night of the spring term, balancing my slipper on the top of the frame of the dormitory's open sash window. As I explained to the headmaster the next day, I was doing such a peculiar thing as part of the game of 'truth, dare, kiss, command or promise' which involved accepting a challenge or paying a forfeit. This had been my dare and I was halfway through it when she came in checking on the boys after lights out.

'And, what are *you* doing?'

There was no possible answer to this question, so I gave none. Inviting me to put on my dressing gown and follow her, she took me to the study door of the school's deputy headmaster. When he appeared she briefly explained that I was out of bed playing the fool after lights out.

The obligatory lecture on why I must be beaten was at least mercifully brief.

'The fact that it's the last night of term but one does not excuse your wilful breaking of the school rules about not being out of bed after lights out. If I don't beat you tonight, then we will have anarchy in the school tomorrow night. Take off your dressing gown and lie over the bed.'

He began to hit me with his leather slipper. It hurt like hell and by the third stroke I was fighting back tears. These, however, I kept soundless as the unwritten schoolboy code of conduct demanded. By wiping my face on the counterpane just before getting up, I even contrived to appear relatively dry-eyed. Mercifully he stopped after four strokes rather than the conventional six.

I then received an apology. 'I'm genuinely sorry to do that to you because on the whole you're a good and bright lad. Please don't make me have to do it to you again.'

She was waiting outside to lead me back up the stairs to my dormitory. She was wearing not only her customary short skirt and high heels, but a pair of fashionable, white fishnet tights as she climbed the stairs in front of me. The skirt was slightly flared and swished enticingly around her thighs, while the high heels enhanced the length of her smooth, slim legs. With my bottom still throbbing painfully, I followed her, entranced by the view and wondering whether this walk might have been worth the pain.

Arriving back at my dormitory, she turned and smiled. 'You're a nice lad, so please stay in bed from now on.'

The beating had a lasting effect on me. Once I was back in bed, my hand seemed drawn to my penis which, apparently of its own accord, seemed to have become erect. As I stroked myself, images of recent events whirled unbidden in my mind, though roles seemed somehow to have changed.

Now it was she who was beating me; she seemed to have lost her suit and be in her underwear; now she was naked and I was beating her; she rather than my hand was playing with me. The kaleidoscope of images grew ever faster. Finally, I came for the first time. I remembered that I was sufficiently able to keep the noise to a minimum, but the pattern of my adolescent fantasies had been set.

* * *

Over the next three months, I visit the Leonora Club half a dozen times. Although I see her, I never sleep with Kate who so attracted me on my first visit but, advised by the fixer, I enjoy a delightful, tall, slim, blonde Swede. It is, however, my second visit which yields the most amusement.

I have planned the visit carefully. Earlier in the evening I address the supper club of an Oxford contemporary, now an MP. It is part of what is often called the 'rubber chicken circuit', about forty of the party faithful in a village hall.

I tell H that I will be staying over at my parents and tell my father that he has to cover for me if necessary, but actually that I am going to spend the night with a working girl. As we have always been close, he is well aware of my doings and I regularly entertain him with stories of my experiences.

After the inevitable raffle, the MP drops me with his thanks at the station in time for the last train to London.

I'm in the Leonora Club by 11 p.m. and the fixer says that my Swede is not there, but there is a woman who he thinks will suit me rather well.

A long pink dress adorns a tall, slim body below a finely featured face and short curly hair. Her skin is pale brown and she must have a combination of white and black blood in her.

There is no hint of awkwardness as she joins me and we begin to talk. Once she knows I'm involved in politics, she tells me, 'I don't much approve of all this.'

'So why on earth do you work here?'

'Because I have to. I did work in insurance IT, but I was made redundant and I have to pay the mortgage and the school fees.'

'This is fascinating. Go on.'

'My son goes to an independent school and I do this so I can afford it.'

As we are having a nice chat I decide to take things further. 'Look, you can't sit here much longer without me buying champagne,' I point out. 'I like you so, if I buy some, will you come back to my hotel? I assume three hundred pounds is OK?'

'Yes, that's fine. Will you buy me some cigarettes as well?'

Transactions complete, she tells me all about the place from the perspective of the working girl. The manager is generally OK but something of a dictator; stay on his right side and you're fine, annoy him and you're in trouble: which means out.

By this stage the floor show has begun and I watch it surreptitiously, for it would be rude for my attention to stray from her, at least too obviously. Besides, she is more to my taste than the stripper.

An hour or so later, with the champagne gone, I ask if it's time to leave.

The engaging man at reception takes care of the administration, booking us into the hotel and providing the driver to take us there.

Up to this point I have scarcely touched her, but the long brown limbs and slim torso revealed when she slips off the long pink dress are all I have hoped. Our lovemaking is slow and lazy as we mix talking, caressing, sucking and kissing.

She slips away at about 3 a.m. I sleep at the hotel and have breakfast before going on to a one-day conference on the future of aviation policy, where I have a word with the civil servants behind the government's white paper and put across the case against one particular development. So I help the taxpayer by stopping a new civilian airport being built on their doorstep. In return they pick up my hotel bill.

FOURTEEN

'I begin to behave like the clichéd middle-aged lover with his young mistress'

The local paper again supplies the phone number of an establishment, carefully selected to be close enough for easy access and distant enough that I am not 'shitting on my own doorstep'. It is an entirely undistinguished Tudor-bethan semi on one of the late 1930s arterial dual carriage-ways which once speeded but now impede the flow of London's traffic.

Once checked out through the spyhole in the door, I am ushered in. The maid puts me into a typical lounge complete with reproduction coffee table and burgundy Dralon® velvet sofa. She gives me a price list whilst telling me that there are two girls for me to choose from. I notice that the price list offers a bubble bath and full sex for £70, an option I have not had before.

While I am noting this, the first girl presents herself. Dressed in bra and pants, she is a perfectly reasonable five-foot-four-ish, curvy, brunette 'girl next door'. I await the second.

A couple of minutes later, there framed in the doorway is a doll-like vision of loveliness so much to my taste that I can hardly believe it.

'The second one, please,' I say to the maid when she returns, my voice slightly hoarse and almost strangled in my throat by the physical perfection (at least to my eyes) of what I am about to have.

She returns. She is five-foot-eight or so, size eight, with no chest to speak of and long, coltish limbs. Her skin is flawless with no apparent moles, marks or blemishes. Her face is pretty, like that of a china doll with large eyes, small nose and even, perfectly proportioned features; the complexion is, like her skin, incredible in its flawlessness. She says I can call her Trisha.

''Ello. What you gonna 'ave then?'

'I thought I might try the bubble bath. I've not had one of those before.'

This is not quite true as H and I having been having baths together for years but I decide that they don't count.

Trisha takes me to a good-sized double bedroom and invites me to undress while she goes to run the bath. She comes back, gives me a fluffy white towel and invites me to climb in. As she follows me into the suds, I notice that she is, indeed, very flat-chested, but has nice nipples whilst her slit is smooth and shaven in a Brazilian. Almost immediately her mobile goes. She climbs out, glances at the number and comes back leaving it unanswered.

'Aren't you going to answer it?'

'Nah, it's my boyfriend an' we're rowin'.'

'What about?'

'I've dumped him 'cause he's been unfaithful to me. An' now 'e wants me back.'

I laugh and she knows why, for whatever else this woman is, she is certainly not stupid.

'This don't count. This is work.'

'Does he know what you do?'

''E knows I work 'ere but 'e thinks I'm like the maid. 'E doesn't know I do this.'

'What if he were to find out?'

''E'd 'ave a real go at me but it wouldn't be fair, I wouldn't deserve it 'cause it's the only way I can earn any money an' I've got two kids to look after.'

'You're joking,' I objected. 'You don't look old enough to have had two kids and your figure is just wonderful, it's simply not that of a mother of two.'

''Ow old d'you think I am?'

'Nineteen, twenty, twenty-one?'

'I'm twenty-four.'

'You can't be.'

'I've always looked young. Lots of my customers wan' me to dress up as a schoolgirl, the disgustin' pervs.'

I make a mental note.

During all this time, I am taking in the beauty of her as we sit facing one another in the bath, her at the less comfortable end with the taps. Her legs are between mine and I stroke them, noting their complete smoothness.

'You have quite the most wonderful skin.'

'Lots of blokes say that. Makes me feel like a freak sometimes, as if I'm not normal or somethin'. The water's gettin' cold. We'd be'er get aht.'

As she does, the mobile rings and again her boyfriend gets no answer.

'He's not going to leave you alone.'

'Oh, this 'as bin goin' on since Tuesday. He left 'is mobile an' it went off an' there was this woman who rang off when I answered so I looked at 'is calls an' 'er number came up all the time an' when 'e came back for the phone I asked 'im who she was an' 'e told me to mind me own business an' I said, "You've bin screwin' 'er, ain't ya?" an' 'e wouldn't answer so I told 'im to fuck off. That was Sunday an' then 'e begins callin' me an' 'e's bin doin' so ever since even at night so I 'ave to switch the phone off but in this business 'e knows I can't do that so it's all a big pain.'

'So what are you going to do?'

'Jus' go on ignorin' 'im till 'e gets the message.'

Having towelled herself dry, she invites me out and begins to dry me. This is fairly cursory.

'Finish yourself off an' then come through to the bedroom.'

When I do, she is lying on the bed in a basque and stockings looking simply ravishing.

'You're quite beautiful, you know. With your figure and looks you really ought to be on a catwalk.'

'Yeah, well, I'm too old now an' I've got the kids so it wouldn't work. D'you want a massage?'

'That would be very nice.'

I lie naked on the bed. She puts talc on my back and rubs it in. The phone rings again but she completely ignores it this time.

'Roll over.'

Talc is now put on my stomach and my hands begin to explore her body. At this point, I notice a large mole on her leg. She does have a blemish and I think I recall reading somewhere that the quantity of moles is genetically fixed but their distribution is individual. If so, all hers must have come together, but it is scarcely visible and complete perfection is impossible.

By now, I am impressively priapic so she rolls on a condom.

''Ow do you want me?'

'Every possible conceivable way, but let's start with you on top, as I always believe that the woman should be on top.'

As we dress afterwards I ask her about her children.

'The boy's six an' 'e's all right but my girl she's three an' lovely but a right little madam. She goes to nursery school an' they keep tellin' 'er off an' makin' 'er cry an' I tell 'em to leave my kid alone. I'm not 'avin' anyone messin' 'er around.'

As I leave I check out what days she works because I know I am coming back just as soon as I can. When I get home and am pouring a drink for us, H asks, 'How was your day?'

'Not at all bad, really not bad at all.'

The second time I see Trisha is the very next time she is working, for I am smitten. Again we take a bath. We catch up on the boyfriend.

''E came round an' I wouldn't let 'im in so 'e smashed the glass in me door an' I 'ad to threaten to call the police.'

'I suppose he wants to see the children.'

'Oh, the kids aren't 'is. No, they're from my previous relationship.'

'So he's not their father?'

'No. I 'aven't seen their father for a couple of years now. Anyway, as 'e's leavin', 'e shouts that if I'm not careful 'e'll 'ave me done for benefit fraud.'

'Are you worried?'

'Nah, 'cause 'e rips off people's credit cards an' if 'e tries to do me, I can run 'im in to the police so we've each got somethin' on each other. I phoned 'im to make sure 'e remembered this. Only I got that woman again, an' she began ringin' me and threatenin' me.'

'I should just back off, if I were you. Leave them be, though actually I think that he will try to get you back. Certainly I would. You really are quite stunningly beautiful.'

'Not really, I'm not that good lookin', there's loads of girls more beautiful than me.'

'I don't think so.'

As I leave, I know that, as she works twice a week, I will, for the moment at least, see her twice a week. I also ask for and am given her mobile number so I can check that she is working, as I do not wish to see anyone else.

Because her days are Tuesday and Thursday, I have to sandwich my visits between my work and evening political events, meetings like the scrutiny committee on which I am serving or – as happens a couple of weeks later – going to a Conservative Association social to listen to an MP give a speech. The MP in question was then still an MEP and although I am a great admirer of this MP's political acumen I find that switch hard to fathom; given the choice I would rather be a European parliamentarian any day. It's vastly closer to the traditional role of an MP, considering trade or foreign policy rather than serving as the glorified local councillor fixing local drains, which, in my opinion, is what most modern MPs now are.

On that occasion, the invite is 7.30 for 8.00. H is there well before me, as I knew she would be, talking to one of the officials. When I walk in to the association offices, she says, 'We were just wondering where you were and I said that you would walk in at one minute to eight, and you have to the second.'

How well H knows me.

Doing all this takes practical organisation and, over the weeks that follow, I structure my diary very carefully around Trisha. The simplest tactic is to arrange a three o'clock meeting that I know I can finish in less than an hour, and then use the free time to travel out to see her. I experiment between going home to pick up my car and using public transport.

The car, a second one alongside the BMW which is more H's than mine, is a very recent purchase and appeals to my sense of humour. At a planning committee a few months ago I was offered a lift by the Labour chair. He showed me to a 4-litre Jaguar and I couldn't resist a crack: 'Is emulating John "two Jags" Prescott now compulsory for the aspiring Labour politician?'

'It was my father's until he died a few months ago. I'm probably going to sell it.'

'No promises but if you decide to, let me know as I may be interested.'

A couple of months later, it is mine for a price so low that nobody believes it if I tell them: because it is a large Jaguar with a personalised number plate, it creates an illusion of affluence which belies the fact that it is nearly fifteen years old with nearly 150,000 miles on the clock. It is, however, in beautiful condition.

Again, that issue of illusion and reality: Trisha is certainly impressed, though not remotely surprised, when she learns what I drive!

I, meanwhile, learn even more about her.

With her figure she was a good runner and her father used to train with her until her parents split up. Then her father effectively deserted her and the running stopped. Although she is still in touch with him, they don't speak as often as she'd like. Her mother had a new partner with whom Trisha did not get on so she was kicked out when she was just fifteen. She was taken in by a bloke who made her pregnant twice and then, in turn, left her.

Trisha tells me that the place where we meet is shutting down. The insight into the system is interesting. Neighbours have been watching and taking photographs of the comings and goings. (Will that include me? I experience a frisson of fear.) They complain to the police, who tip off the owner, actually the landlord, that if it continues they will have to act. So the place shuts, quietly and without fuss. The local community – I picture middle-aged and elderly women peering from behind their curtains – is satisfied, order is maintained and it merely requires the working girls to find another venue. This, however, is not easy and Trisha says that she cannot easily see me.

I approach a friend and ask if I can borrow his flat. He agrees and this is where Trisha and I start meeting.

Having fixed my work schedule, we greet one another mid-afternoon at the almost deserted nearby Tube station.

In contrast with my business suit, her cowboy boots, skintight jeans, tiny T-shirt and denim jacket all make me think 'trailer trash' and it must be obvious to the couple of staff on duty what is going on. I decide to give them their money's worth, embracing her warmly and kissing her on the lips.

'You know this is the first time I've seen you with clothes on.'

She laughs and starts talking away at me about the complexities of organising baby-sitting. I love this for sometimes I just want to listen.

At the flat it is cold and though I put the heating on it takes a while to have an effect, so we go straight to bed with the bottle of fizz I have brought. She complains of the cold so we make love fast for warmth but then stay in bed drinking the wine.

I love this slim, athletic body and simply spend time caressing and fondling it just like I once did with H, who says that I will never get enough physical affection because my mother didn't stroke me enough as a child.

Here there are no time pressures, so an hour or so later we have sex for a second time. As we dress I slip her £100, asking if it is enough, which she says it is. Then I propose we go the short distance to the nearest bar, a gentrified gastro-pub.

It is still only about five o'clock and we are the only customers. She asks for vodka and Red Bull®, but afterwards switches to the bottle of wine I have bought. We go back to the subject of her father, who has promised to ring her but failed to do so.

'Why don't you ring him?'

'But 'e said 'e'd ring me an' 'e ought to.'

'How long ago?'

'Eh?'

'How long ago was he supposed to ring you? I mean today, two days ago, last week?'

'Yesterday.'

'And he's probably aware that he hasn't and now feels guilty but can't bring himself to do it because of the guilt, so why don't you make it easy for him and make the call? You'll feel better, he'll feel better and you have nothing to lose. There's no downside to this. Because whatever the outcome, you won't be worse off, so just do it.'

She takes my advice. I don't really listen to the conversation but watch her, seeing the relief on her face and the tears in her eyes when they communicate.

'There you are, you see. You feel better now. What you need to do is think about things from the other person's point of view, work out what they are thinking and feeling and then respond in the way which brings about the outcome you want.'

'I don't understan' 'alf of what you say but I love listening to ya.'

I buy us both a steak.

She has to go at about seven. She phones a taxi, which we share, continuing to cuddle until I give her twenty pounds for the fare and have myself dropped off close to my home. The driver calls me 'boss' and is clearly amused as I see him watching us in his rear-view mirror.

This new arrangement now becomes regular and our intimacy grows in every way. As a couple we are head-turners, for the heels she wears add to the fact that she is in any case a couple of inches taller than me.

I sit in meetings at the House of Commons and in the City fantasising about her and thinking of the next time I will see her, for she is stealing my heart. I begin to behave like the clichéd middle-aged lover with his young mistress, buying her presents.

As Valentine's Day is approaching, I leave a meeting at the Commons, stroll down Victoria Street and go into La Senza.

'Can I help you, sir?'

'Not at the moment, I'm just looking.'

Ten minutes or so later, I am by the till.

'Can I giftwrap them for you, sir?'

I smile.

'Separately, please.'

I am certain that the assistant has noticed that one is size eight and the other size twelve. I see that the packages will be identical.

'Can you hang on a moment, please.'

Taking out a pen, I write an all but invisible 'H' on one and an equivalent 'T' on the other.

The next time we meet, Trisha puts on the baby-doll I bought her to climb into bed with me and tells me that now I am her only lover – and source of additional income beyond her benefits. Thus reassured, I do something I have wanted to do for quite some time but have held back through fear of catching something. I slip down the bed and go down on her, exploring her folds of flesh with my tongue, teasing her until she puts her hands into my armpits, hauls me up, hastily rolls on a condom and pulls me into her.

We part at around seven and this time I make my way to the restaurant where I am taking out H.

She is wearing her present, red silk that can serve either as a top or as an ultra-short nightie. When we get home, she keeps it on to go to bed and adds the white hold-up stockings she knows I really like. As we make love, I make to go down on her but she indicates that she does not want this by putting her hands in my armpits and pulling me into her.

As I fall asleep, I think: one of the best days of my entire life.

I know I am affecting Trisha in all sorts of ways for she tells me about an experience when she was clubbing, and says that when she was about to get into a drunken catfight, 'I tried to think what you'd do, knew it wasn't worth it an' walked away.'

A cloud reappears for she tells me her boyfriend is back on the scene and his mother, who works in the local housing office, is threatening to have her evicted.

'Leave it with me.'

I ring a political contact and good friend of mine who I think will be able to give me some advice.

'I've got a bit of a problem with which you will, I hope, be able to help me. A single parent I know who is a housing association tenant on benefit is being threatened. It's rather unpleasant, effectively blackmail. Without giving you any detail at this stage, if I ask you to intervene, will you do so?'

'Bit difficult to say without knowing any of the detail, but in principle, I don't see why not.'

The next time I see her, I say, 'Simply tell his mother that you've got a protector and if she tries to carry out her threat, she will find that she loses her job.'

The problem goes away, at least for the moment.

We discuss her future.

'I wanna be a beautician, but it's too late.'

I have a very attractive blonde hairdresser to whom I give occasional business advice and help as a councillor, so I consult her.

'I've got this constituent, she came to my surgery. She's a single mum living on benefit but she wants to be a beautician. How can I help her?'

'You're so nice, you know. She needs to do a course at her local college.'

But after I have spoken with the college and the benefits people, all the time posing as a councillor helping a constituent, I discover that Trisha is that bit too old. She's literally just about to pass the cut-off birthday.

She tells me that organising weekday baby-sitting for when we meet up is becoming difficult. However, my friend's flat is not available at weekends. She says she will try to arrange to borrow the flat of a friend, and I can pick her up at her house and drive her round.

As it's not always convenient to speak to each other on the phone, I learn how to text. Hitherto it is not a facility I have needed to use much – most people of my age use the phone, including a mobile, to make calls. As we exchange texts I learn a new language and my thumbs become faster and more adept.

'i cant make it 2nite how about sat?'

'cu at 4.'

'cant really talk but dats fine x.'

'ok 4 sat?'

'sorry hunny cant do it.'

With these exchanges, I gather that we will have to rearrange. I also learn the excitement, the churn of the stomach when a text arrives which I know will be from her. Are we on or are we off?

It is a new medium to raise expectation, dash it and see it raised again.

The next time, we fail in a different way. I drive to her house to pick her up. The house is everything I expected – and feared. It is relatively modern, an enclave of social housing amidst bottom-end mortgage-paying owner-occupiers. The reason for the fear is the complete lack of care it conveys. The long, unmown patches of grass at the front alternating with patches of bare earth, contrasts with the well-kept squares of some of its neighbours. A broken pane in a window of the front door has been hastily boarded over. Another has obviously been repaired but the new beading is unpainted. It all needs sprucing up but I suspect she simply doesn't care, at least not enough to do anything about it.

I knock and wait.

She pulls me in quickly, anxious for us not to be seen. Inside is just like outside. The place is untidy, with dirty crockery in the kitchen, and children's toys strewn all around. Even so, the place conveys an impression of emptiness and I remember how she told me that the boyfriend, though whether she means the current one or a predecessor I am not sure, stole lots of her stuff.

'Sorry, but me baby-sitter's let us down.'

We talk a bit about how and when we can meet and I put my arms around her, fondling and kissing her. On the stairs, her son appears.

'That looks like bein' lovey.'

We pull apart guiltily.

'I'd better go.'

From the car, I text: 'Not cross shit happens ring text me xx.'

Will it be third time lucky?

A week later, we repeat the plan, only this time it works. We are soon sitting on the sofa in a house a few roads away consuming Cava and pistachios I have supplied. The house is like her own but better furnished and tidier.

'So, tell me about your friend?'

'She's like me, she used to do what I do but now she just lives on benefit. Also she doesn't like blokes any more, she's lesbian.'

I see a photograph of a pretty blonde with a bloke and smile.

'She doesn't look much like a lesbian to me.'

'She's into women now 'cause blokes always let ya down.'

Blokes may, but sex with Trisha does not. Upstairs in her friend's double bed we make love and I wonder why and how my life became such that its greatest pleasure is illicit sex with a benefit-defrauding single mother who would appal almost everybody who knows me. And yet I don't give a stuff what anyone thinks about this relationship.

We agree a similar arrangement for the following Saturday.

This time my explanation to my wife is different. On previous occasions, I have supposedly been watching a London rugby team that I support. This Saturday, however, they are playing away from home so a different excuse is needed.

Fortunately the Conservative party can supply it. I go out delivering 'In Touch', the party's intermittent newsletter. I will do this for a couple of hours from ten a.m. until noon and then slip away to see my lover.

As I am about to leave, a text arrives: 'Go 2 hers.'

I do this but no one is there so I drive the short distance to Trisha's.

I park the Jag a hundred yards or so from her house, walk the final distance and ring the bell.

As it remains unanswered, I ring it again.

It is opened by a man and I ask for Trisha.

'Who the fuck are you?'

That, I think, in all the circumstances, is a really good question. And I realise my idiocy fifteen seconds too late.

'No, no, it doesn't matter.'

'So who the fuck are you?'

I begin to back away, wondering whether he is about to attack me. I dare not move too quickly for to do so will have guilt written all over it.

To my relief he disappears back inside whilst I walk briskly back to the car.

Once I reach it, I am shaking so badly I can hardly get out my keys, put them in the lock and start the ignition. As a result, I see him reappear but this time he's dragging Trisha out of the house.

She is wearing only a short dressing gown and I think how lovely she looks even in these circumstances.

He calls out, 'You want 'er, 'ere she is, come an' get 'er.'

I know at this point with cast-iron certainty that I am seeing her for the last time.

As I drive away, tears are in my eyes and my legs are shaking, for I know that I have blown it, our relationship is over, that I do love her and I think that in her way she loves me. My last glimpse of her is through the rear-view mirror with him shouting after me whilst he roughly holds her upper arm.

When I get home, H asks me how the canvassing went. I laugh and say, 'It had its moments but you know how tedious I find these things these days.'

But actually all I want to do is cry and phone her. Two hours later, when H has gone shopping, I do.

'Are you all right? He didn't hit you or anything, did he?'

'Nah, 'e didn't 'it me but he asked me abaht you an' it all came aht, an' you are responsible for the worst day of my entire life.'

'Look, I'm really sorry.'

'Why the 'ell didn't ya just say, "Sorry, wrong address"?'

'I have been wondering that exact question myself. I really wish I had. I'm truly sorry. I just didn't think because I wasn't expecting a man, you see, I –'

'For a bloke who's supposed to be really clever, you're not very bright.'

'I know. I'm sorry. I suppose that's it, then?'

''E's told me I'm never to see ya again.'

'I was afraid of that. Will you?'

'I don't know. I'll think abaht it an' let ya know.'

'Can I call you Monday?'

'Yeah, OK.'

To make matters worse, I am due to speak at my local Conservative Association that night. As I make my way there, all my concentration is on Trisha, as I know it will be all evening. I really wish I did not have to do this. The audience will consist, almost exclusively, of middle-aged and elderly women and a sprinkling of ambitious young men – of which I was once one.

Understanding these two groups is the key to understanding the modern Conservative party.

Elderly women are fearful – of illness, crime, loss of income, their children and grandchildren's welfare and prospects and, associated with all this, the moral decline of society.

The young men know this, so they mould their opinions – in public at least – to appeal to this group who form the majority of any Tory selection committee. Thus the party becomes the hanging, shooting and flogging party.

Once, all this mildly amused me. Now that my ambitions have died, it increasingly irritates and bores me.

At the converted large Victorian house which forms the Association offices, the evening's banalities begin. Fortunately I can do this on autopilot so I set about smiling in the right places, inquiring about the health of grandchildren and maintaining my image of intelligent rectitude. Inwardly I want to cry, because I know I will never make love to Trisha again.

My speech is well received and I finish with a poignant quote from a writer I hold in high esteem.

As I read this to them tears of emotion are in my eyes. They think they are to do with what I am reading: little do they know.

My father has always told me, 'Get back behind the wheel after crashing.' He applied this theory literally once, for he made me do this when I scraped his car shortly after passing my test.

On the Monday, Trisha rings to confirm my dismissal. I control myself, briefly invent a meeting and cry as I travel to a place I have been three or four times before.

The lady is older than some I have frequented but thoroughly expert in what she does, which is turn me on. In fact, the correlation between appearance and sexual excellence is tenuous at best. She's in her late 30s and I like her.

She has told me her story, which seems not uncommon of a certain type. She's fairly middle class with a daughter at private school. Her husband simply walked out on her one day and, in time, failed to make the agreed monthly payments. Whereas some women have the time and means to pursue the husband through the courts or can go on benefits, a woman like her is immediately plunged into a nightmare where she loses too much too quickly: the house because mortgage payments are not kept up, and the daughter's education because school fees have to be paid.

She goes 'on the game' as she calls it, and goes to great lengths to conceal it from everyone she knows. She works in London from about 11 a.m., the earliest most punters want to, till about 8 p.m. – the kind of hours which can offer the appearance of normal commuting.

I know I can trust her, both generally – she knows who I am and we have discussed politics, in which she votes Conservative – and to provide what I need on this occasion.

When I arrive I tell her, 'I am upset.'

'Want to tell me about it?'

'Not really. It doesn't matter.'

'Would you like a glass of wine?'

'That would be really nice.'

And because we share similar outlook and backgrounds and she knows I notice these things, she pours us both a decent claret and I end up telling her about it.

She tells me I am daft, sits upon my knee and kisses me properly on the lips, our tongues teasing one another. This is rare. Many working girls will not allow any form of kissing – it is an intimacy which can be reserved for their boyfriends, or for no one, even when other things are not.

We move to the bed.

With most women, over a period of time you evolve something of a routine – there are only so many variations and you come to know what works between you. Perhaps that is part of the reason I have come to her, because I know I can trust the routine to work.

She, however, is an intelligent woman and able to interpret and understand my needs better than I do myself. Thus when we reach the stage at which I would expect to roll from lying on my stomach over onto my back, she says, 'Not this time, stay where you are.'

And, of course, I obey.

She lies full-length on top of me and her body slithers entrancingly over mine, letting me feel her entire weight. Lubricated by the massage oil she has been applying to my back and legs, I experience a sense of warmth and fellow feeling that is at once sexually arousing and comforting.

She shifts slightly to the left so I can still feel the weight of her breasts on my back and of her thighs on my left leg but giving her access to my anus. Lubricant topped up, she then begins to massage the crack of my bottom. This continues for what seems like ages but is probably only moments – I lose all sense of time. Soothed by the sensation, I scarcely notice the moment of entry, only really feeling her index finger when it has penetrated me to its full length and her knuckles are pressing into my buttocks. It is withdrawn, but only for one finger to become two, which then prod and massage my prostate.

Without her having touched my penis, I notice I am fully erect.

After a while, she withdraws, rolls me over, applies the necessary condom, impales herself upon me and leans forward so I can feel the weight of her on me but this time on my chest. I clasp her to me, her breasts squashed into me. She kisses me while riding me, for all the world having achieved a missionary fuck with her on top.

My coming is noisy and protracted but I think that this time for once she might have come too, for she shudders, her breathing heavy.

Afterwards, as she is still without further customers, we finish the bottle of wine until one appears.

I can only say a genuinely grateful 'thank you'.

I have just emerged and am walking down the street when a voice says to me, 'Hello, and how are you?'

'Oh, hi, not bad and how are you?'

As we catch up I am devoutly hoping that he will not ask

me where I have just come from. For the man I have run into is an ex-MP. It's rather a close call.

A couple of weeks later, I sit down and write an article on public policy – a passage from which reads:

> If you condemn single mothers living on welfare with children by multiple fathers, you should ask if the mother's behaviour is not an entirely rational response to the incentives offered by the state system. Any local councillor asked by an unqualified seventeen-year-old, 'Wouldn't I be better off getting pregnant?' knows that the honest answer is 'yes'.
>
> Not only is she incentivised not to live with a man, she is also incentivised either not to work or to work in the black economy, probably in the sex industry. Why?
>
> Working legally reduces her benefit at a very high marginal tax rate and other benefits also disappear. This poverty trap draws her towards the black economy in ways few can resist. Not only can she keep all she earns without losing benefit, it also offers flexibility. Importantly for childcare, she can work hours convenient to her.
>
> For an unqualified, attractive woman, the highest pay for the least work in the most flexible working conditions means the sex industry.

When it is finished, I circulate the full-length version amongst a small group of mildly influential friends and allies to challenge their complacency about the system we help to run. They privately agree but believe little can be done.

I reflect that with Trisha I have not only hurt myself and perhaps her, but my experience with her and what I have learned about her life is another step in the process by which I am falling out of love with everything, the values, the institutions, the party and the people I am supposed to hold dear. I am increasingly contemptuous of the smug self-satisfaction and self-righteousness of all that is 'respectable'.

FIFTEEN

'My fantasies have just been realised in the flesh'

I meet a friend, a merchant banker who works in the City, in the City Boot wine bar. As well as being convenient, being situated right by one of the exits from Moorgate Tube station, it reproduces a nineteenth-century wood-panelled interior in the late twentieth-century Barbican development. The juxtaposition and incongruity amuse me. It's as if to say that no interior from the building's own century will do in creating the right atmosphere.

My friend is also a politician and that is why I am seeing him. He is advising me on the best way to influence a committee, of which he used to be chairman but is now no longer a member. I will pay for the lunch and he will declare the hospitality. No impropriety is involved.

I give him a copy of the briefing note I have prepared. He reads through it.

'Fine. Don't bother with the last sentence, it's syco-phantic, but apart from that use it exactly as is. Now are you going to buy me a second bottle or do we go for port?'

I opt for the port, but only a glass for I have in my pocket a card picked from a telephone box en route for a place near Old Street I have decided to sample. I am still getting over Trisha and am therefore seeking out new haunts unsullied by her memory.

Three-quarters of an hour or so later I am standing outside a modern terraced house, though built in a retro style, several roads to the north of the station. The terrace itself appears almost out of place, surrounded by office buildings. It is presumably an attempt to bring residents to what is effectively a business district, but what it has actually done, in at least one case, is provide the premises for a new service of which I am about to partake.

By now I am familiar with procedure. The maid, a chatty and friendly soul who I like, ushers me into a bedroom. There I wait and, when nobody immediately appears, I take off my jacket, sit down on the one chair, take out *How The Mind Works* and begin to read it.

A few minutes later, a vision enters the room. My fantasies have just been realised in the flesh. She is six feet tall, though she stoops slightly because she knows that the vast majority of men want to be taller than the woman. She has black hair with a subtle touch of auburn in it, the highest cheek bones I can ever recall, sharp eyes made more piercing by blue eye-shadow, a very slightly flattened nose, a delicate mouth and a body straight off the catwalk. Half to her and half to myself, I say, 'You're gorgeous.'

'What are you reading?'

I show her the cover page. She takes the book off me and reads the publisher's blurb, which tells her that it is a thoroughly serious piece of work: over 800 pages by Steven Pinker, the professor of cognitive neuroscience at Massachusetts Institute of Technology.

I learn her name – or, at least the one she is using: Mimi. She claims to be Spanish, to which I say, 'I don't think so.'

'What do you mean you don't think so?'

'I mean that you don't strike me as Spanish. Prove it – speak some Spanish to me.'

She laughs.

'I come from wherever the customer wants me to come from or wherever my mood takes me. I have whatever name I like and I change it when I want to. Who do you want me to be?'

'I want you to be who you really are and to come from wherever you actually come from.'

Again, she laughs.

'That's not your business. You're too curious but I'm Russian, though now you won't know whether you can believe anything I say.'

'I won't, of course, but I can judge whether I believe you.'

We agree her price, £80 for half an hour, and she goes out to put the money away, leaving me almost trembling with anticipation. I have found the pages of *Vogue* brought to life with a brain, imagination and humour.

I go back to my book but stare at it blankly, seeing only her as I wait.

When she comes back, she is direct.

'Why you reading this book?'

'I'm trying to answer the only question worth answering, why people are as they are. I'm trying to discover what makes human nature tick.'

She says nothing for a moment but looks pensive.

'Take off your clothes.'

As I obey the order, she says, 'So tell me, does your book explain why people do things which damage them?'

'Why do you ask?'

'Do you always answer question with another question?'

'Often enough, yes, because my answer depends upon the reason I am being asked. I can't give an appropriate, interesting answer without knowing the motivation behind the question.'

'My boyfriend, he is idiot. He does things to piss me off, which he knows will piss me off, yet he still does them and I want to know why.'

'Well, the book sort of gives an answer. It explains that, driven as we are by imperatives given by our genes, what looks irrational behaviour from an obvious perspective, can actually be entirely sensible if viewed as the genes' attempt to maximise their chances of reproduction. This can explain altruism, which is not actually altruistic; sacrifice, which can appear daft; and suicidal depression, which appears totally insane. So it can explain actions which appear self-damaging.'

'But that does not explain my boyfriend.'

'It's probably about comfort patterns. We all acquire in infancy and childhood experiences which we come to feel comfortable with because we are used to them, so we go on repeating them even when they are damaging. Your boyfriend's behaviour probably goes back to his relationship with his mother.'

'Lie down – on your stomach.'

She begins to massage my back.

'My boyfriend, he is *wanker*. He argues with me when he knows it will make me cross so I kick him out and won't let him see me, but he goes on behaving in the same way.'

'So why does he do these things?'

'That's what I am asking you.'

'Perhaps he's just stupid. Have you read *Men are from Mars, Women are from Venus*?'

'I have read this book.'

'Well, get your boyfriend to read it.'

'Ha, I have tried, you see, but he is *wanker* so he won't read it. Roll over.'

I gaze at her stunningly beautiful face, smile and win one in return. It is the first and it is ravishing.

'If you have asked him to read it and he refuses this request from someone as gorgeous as you, he *is* a wanker, a complete idiot. I would, I did and I gave it to my wife.'

'Ha, you have wife but you come to places like this so you can't be that clever!'

'My wife gave me permission to be here, at least not specifically here today with you, but in general terms she has agreed to my having sex with other women.'

'This I do not believe.'

'Well, it happens to be true, we talked about it, she wants us to remain married but my libido is stronger than hers and she finds me too demanding, so this is the arrangement we have agreed. It may be a compromise but it suits us both.'

'Ha, typical man, you mean it suits you and your wife puts up with it because she has to but she will not like it.'

'I promise you she doesn't mind. She –'

I can no longer talk because exquisite sensations are driving all conversation from my mind and neither can she speak for, having dressed me in a condom, her tongue is rolling up and down my penis. I put my hand inside the front of her thong and begin to play with her. She doesn't stop me but increases the tempo of her tongue. It is my intention at a certain point to get her to stop so I can have proper sex with her, but the oral experience is so wonderful that I never get around to asking. I come into the condom in her mouth.

At that point, most women stop. She does not. She goes on using her tongue and hand to the point where pleasure begins to turn to pain. I cry out hysterically, thresh my legs and head and then, as I come down, open my eyes to see her laughing at me.

She cleans me with a baby wipe, appropriately enough because she has reduced me to a babyish loss of all physical control. I know from this moment that I am putty in her hands, manipulable by her more or less at will. She has made me so sensitive that the action of the baby wipe induces further tremors like the aftershocks of an earthquake.

'I absolutely completely must see you again.'

'I am here Wednesdays and Fridays.'

'Even so, please can I have your mobile number?'

She thinks for a moment or two and then dictates it to me.

'That was one of the best experiences of my entire life.'

I see her laughing at me as I go to kiss her. Her own lips avoid mine as she turns first one cheek then the other.

As I walk away, I know that I simply have to see this woman again.

The following Wednesday I try to. The bell remains stubbornly unanswered despite repeated pressing. I ring her mobile.

'I have same experience. I turn up and no answer. I don't know why it happen.'

'When and where can I see you?'

'I think about this and let you know. Ring me tomorrow.'

'What time?'

'About midday.'

At twelve noon precisely I am ringing her phone.

'Now is not convenient, ring me this afternoon.'

At 3.30 p.m., she says, 'You can see me Tuesday.'

She gives me an address in Cleveland Street close to the Post Office Tower, which is how I still think of it despite BT's attempts to christen it the Telecom Tower.

I go at lunch time, having arranged a meeting at the Commons that morning. Mimi's house number, at least what I have written down, does not appear to exist. Ridiculously I am loath to ring her because I do not wish to appear incompetent. My wife has told me that she married me for my competence, a reason which, in the opinion of certain friends, if true means that she has never really loved me. I do not believe this but can see the logic of the argument. Whatever the case, it means that, more perhaps than most men, I never like to appear incompetent in the eyes of women I love.

I am forced to call, though, and learn that I need to add a hundred, which takes me to the northern end and a three-storey nineteenth-century house. It has a red light outside and its virtually identical neighbour has a notice saying, 'This is a private residence'. There is a bird-dropping-encrusted, paper-strewn set of wrought iron steps to a disused basement entrance. Aha, I think, for once we are not in the basement, but as soon as I am let in through the front door I discover I am wrong, for the plump, smiling, middle-aged, working-class maid says, 'Down the stairs, to the left,' and ushers me to a modern pine interior staircase which takes me down into the basement.

The room itself is as I have now come to expect. Not recently decorated, the walls are strewn with the uniforms of the trade: nurse, schoolgirl and lingerie items, much of it in the outsizes which indicate that the male customers wish to wear the garments themselves as much as have the working girl wear them. Whips, canes and mirrors complete the clichéd picture, the latter positioned low down to the side of the bed so the customer can attempt to watch himself in action. The lighting is dim, provided by a bedside lamp. There is a single bulb hanging in the centre of the room and I turn this on, for this woman's appearance is something on which I wish to feast my eyes.

This is one venue where you should picture us over the months that follow – on Tuesdays.

On Thursdays, she is near Heathrow. So that is where I manipulate my schedule to enable me to go and see her. The actual locations vary, for the life of many of these establishments can be measured in weeks or months rather than years as neighbours spot them, complain and the police shut them down, only for them quickly to reopen in a similar location nearby.

The Heathrow locations are on the Bath Road, or in Hayes or Harlington. All are low-rise flats or suburban terraces or semis built in the 1960s or 70s.

The relationship very quickly comes to have discernable patterns. One is about light. All these rooms, even the ones in upper-storey flats near Heathrow, tend to be shrouded in darkness. I turn lights on, she turns them off.

When I arrive she always makes me wait so I take out a book. As she walks in she says, 'Reading again? This is not library.'

But she is always interested in what the book is and frequently browses through it. After I have paid, she will say, 'Be ready.'

For she wants me to be lying on the bed, naked, waiting for her.

I very rarely have full sex with her. Instead she uses her mouth relentlessly to blow my mind unfailingly. But above all, we talk, more or less resuming our conversation exactly where it has left off from the time before.

I learn about her, or at least what she chooses to tell me.

Her mother is a teacher and her father an engineer. She is well read – she had read all of Balzac by the age of fourteen – and finds most English people ignorant and stupid. She has a degree and did a variety of jobs after it. She came here fleeing from a relationship. Her then boyfriend was being a demanding pain so she decided at less than 48 hours' notice simply to buy a ticket and run away. In fact she has run away from relationships twice in her life and warns me that if I become too insistent, as most men do, she will run away from me.

She tried Paris first, but entering France was difficult so she came to London – as a student to learn English. She worked in coffee shops and the like to support herself. But, after a few months, one day she simply had no money whatsoever and asked a female friend for help. The friend said, 'I will not give you any money but I will show you how you can get some.'

'How did you find it that first time?'

'Difficult, but I knew I had to do it, so I did and it wasn't so bad.'

'And now?'

'I'm used to it. Most clients are fine and I simply refuse the ones I don't like the look of. They're all ignorant wankers, of course, all men are, but I can manage them.'

'You're allowed to turn them away?'

'If I want to. No mere man makes me do what I don't like.'

'Of course, because the woman is always the chooser. All a man can do is say, "Will you have me?" and the woman decides whether she will or not. Any intelligent man knows that.'

'My boyfriend continues to be *wanker*.'

'Tell me about him.'

'He's Serbian but has EU passport. He fought in Balkans. He picked me up in coffee shop where I worked. We've been together now for nearly three years. He's mechanic but is bouncer at the moment.'

'If you want to know what I think, he's not good enough for you. He knows it and knows that he's going in time to lose you, so subconsciously he's testing you, playing out his own fears to see whether you will dump him.'

'Most men are not intelligent.'

'Maybe, but I am and I understand these things. It's a function of biological role. And next time I see you, I will give you a present which tells you why.'

The following Tuesday, I give her a copy of Jared Diamond's book, *Why Is Sex Fun? The Evolution Of Human Sexuality*.

She looks at it and says, 'I don't believe it. Your first present to me and it's book. My first present from a book.'

Only later do I think about the implications of this remark: her *first* present, which means there will be others, many others, for we both know I am truly and totally intoxicated by her.

Back to the City Boot with the same contact I met a few weeks earlier. He briefs me on the current sentiment amongst his contacts and we work out what arguments I will advance and how I will present them. This time we opt for the extra bottle.

So when I see her I am more than a little pissed. I am frank about the implications: 'You won't find that thing is necessarily of very much use, I'm afraid.'

'So why have you come to see me? What do you want of me?'

In my inebriated state, I say exactly what comes into my head and perhaps even I am surprised at my sentiments. 'I want to live with you. I want to have a child with you and eventually I want to marry you, probably in that order. I love you passionately, I think of you all the time and want to be with you. I would do anything for you.'

'Anything?'

'Yes, anything.'

'Jump out of that window.'

'Now you're being silly.'

'You said anything, but like all men you don't mean it. You require compromises.'

'Not really, but it has to be sensible. I'm not going to jump out of the window because it is not in either of our interests. But actually I would do anything you asked.'

'Ring your wife.'

'No.'

'There, I told you you won't do anything. Give me your phone and tell me your wife's number.'

I do exactly that.

'I'm going to ring it.'

'No, you're not, but that's not because I'm going to stop you. It's because you're a highly intelligent woman and you know that it's not a sensible thing to do. It's not actually in your interests, so you won't do it.'

'I might.'

Instead she goes to work on me but, although I am highly aroused, I cannot come.

'You *wanker*, like all the rest.'

'Yes, I know I am, but at least I agree with you, I'm better than most and I understand why it's the case.'

'You can't understand, you're a man and no man can.'

'I'll prove it to you.'

Seeing as I spend much of my time writing papers on the most inane and dreary matters of local government, I was struck by the idea of preparing one on something of real interest – human relationships. Especially as I was becoming quite well-versed in the sexual form of them. The next time I see her, the following Tuesday, I hand in my essay.

SIXTEEN

'At that moment I would like all three of them'

MIMI MANUSTURBARE

A man goes to his mistress complaining about bourgeois women and their values.

The clever, beautiful Russian replies that men are wankers, literally and figuratively, for it is men who have shaped a world where they screw around but want to marry virgins; let women do all the work and cannot be trusted; want a whore in the bedroom, a cook and cleaner in the kitchen and the perfect mother for their children.

The key to the courtesan's comments is to understand that human beings are part of a family. Close relatives are chimpanzees and bonobos, sharing 98 per cent of human DNA. Both live in troops and are promiscuous. This means no chimp or bonobo father knows his offspring, so there are no specific father–child bonds and no lasting pair bonds.

Male competition is about virility: he whose sperm gets to the egg first wins! This means large, productive penises and testes. It also means the female chooses: at ovulation, she boldly advertises her availability; he offers; she selects.

In humans, women's ovulation is concealed, however, and they do not advertise availability. Men therefore are effectively programmed to look for sex all the time. In principle a man is prepared to be violent, but he also knows a woman may not choose him precisely because he shows himself to be aggressive.

She wants him to be powerful enough to protect her yet caring enough to cherish and help with nine months of pregnancy and years of nurture as she struggles to ensure her children thrive.

For a woman, sex can shape her entire life. For a man, it can be a brief pleasure before he wanders away. Her role forces her to be responsible; his allows him to be irresponsible. However, he has a specific problem.

All women know when they are a mother. By contrast, until DNA testing, no man can ever be sure he is the father. We begin to see humans as they are. Men want lots of sex for themselves but do not want women to enjoy the same freedom. She has to cope with the consequences, children she has to carry, feed, shelter, protect and raise.

In short, she works hard and sex is not the priority for her it is for him – except to keep his services: for, noting his promiscuous nature and assuming she wants him, she has to be regularly available. It is therefore useful if she enjoys sex, so she has her own organ of sexual pleasure – the clitoris.

We begin to see characteristic human behaviour.

Women are selective about when and with whom they have sex. The more in demand she is, in principle the more selective she can be, though a beautiful, clever woman may be in sufficient practical difficulty to have sex with partners she would not otherwise consider.

Men will stick around and help as long as they feel it is worth it but, if the price becomes too high, pursue alternatives: other women, men, or wanking (simple, cheap and available, but perhaps least satisfying!).

Both men and women want a quality partner whose offspring will be successful. Beauty is a means to recognise these characteristics and symmetry and purity of form are universal. However, humans also prize intelligence because, generally, the more intelligent a person, the better their prospects.

Their roles suggest why men prize beauty more than brains whereas women do the reverse. For a woman with her high degree of dependence, intelligence increases the likelihood he will deliver what she needs. Physical beauty is less relevant. By contrast, the male's ability to 'love her and leave her' makes looks more important than brains.

Technology, however, is now changing even this: as modern woman can control her fertility, she can be the architect of her destiny, free of the cycle of pregnancy, birth, lactation and pregnancy again – without being celibate. It means traditional rulebooks, the sexual laws imposed by religion, can be junked – but only, as yet, for Western, educated women with access to contraception. What we are taught as eternal truths are in fact man-made codes created to prevent the inconvenient consequences of female promiscuity (but not male). At long last, in present-day society women can enjoy sex, like men!

I'm particularly pleased with the essay's title. Mimi sees it and smiles. She understands my play on words with her name. Few English people would know that '*manusturbare*' is Latin for 'wanker'. In the subsequent discussion I realise that her Latin is, if anything, rather better than mine. I simply cannot believe this woman; she is surely too good to be true?

I sense that my desires have long since passed beyond pure lust. I am infatuated like the wizards and knights of the pre-Raphaelite posters with which I adorned the walls of my public school study – to the contemptuous amusement of my dumber and cruder contemporaries.

When I tell her this, she opens up to me about her bad side, which she says I have never seen and have to know.

Over the following weeks, she tells me stories. As she does so, I lose all sense of time in her presence. It is a complete escape from everything and everyone else and when I come to leave I tend to have no idea how long I have been there.

'One day, my parents want to go out for evening so tell me I must go stay with my, how you say, granny. I say no. I hate staying with Granny who makes me eat at set time, go to bed at set time, do homework and read books. She runs timetable which I must do and don't like. So I refuse but my father takes me but is walking distance. At first I go along but when it reach certain time, I just leave and go back to my parents' house, and lock door, you know, from inside, so my parents are locked out when they come back and though they try everything to wake me I won't let them in so they must sleep at my granny's so they can see how they like it!'

Another time she tells me, 'When I was twelve, my parents took me to a restaurant. I was pretty girl all dressed up but decided to be bad. It had tomato plants and I decided was more fun throwing tomatoes at other customers. So I sat there throwing these tomatoes and no one could stop me and after that I knew was more fun being bad.'

She continues with another story.

'One day, I have toothache and my mother take me to dentist. I will not let dentist touch me so they hold me down, my father and mother, whilst the dentist tries to begin work but they are not strong enough and I bite. Soon his finger is bleeding but I am also. I get up from chair and I come out screaming with blood all around my mouth like devil. They chase after me but they cannot catch me so I run around streets like devil girl because I am bad.'

'No, you're not, not really. They just didn't handle you right.'

'You have not seen my bad side.'

I ask what it consists of. The answer is far from clear. The best I can deduce is that her traditional attitudes make her job and behaviour shameful, and that when she is upset, she will voice unpleasant truths, shout and scream and throw things.

It reminds me of being in a kitchen aged six watching as my mother verbally berates and throws a knife at my father. There is nothing it seems to me very terrible in all this. It fits with the values with which I was inculcated: as my father taught me, no gentleman ever strikes a woman (consensual, submissive sex excepted, of course); if she seeks to do violence to him he may avoid and even restrain her. I can see my father grasping my mother's knife-wielding arm but he does not strike back. Mimi's values are my own.

'My sister wants to come here and join me. I cannot allow this. I'm not having her caught up in all of this. My mother would never forgive me but she cannot come. They think I work in coffee shop.'

'They must think English wages are high.'

'They have no idea.'

'What's your sister doing, at the moment, I mean?'

'She's at university but this is expensive and I have to help pay. She silly girl who thinks it's boring, thinks it would be more fun over here.'

Instantly, Angela's desire to leave Cambridge comes to mind. I picture the younger sister as some kind of midpoint between these two entrancing, beautiful women with whom I have been stupid enough to fall in love.

'What's she like, your sister?'

'Oh, she's silly girl, she doesn't know what life is like and my parents spoil her because she is baby of family and she was affected by Chernobyl.'

'The fallout? How bad?'

'Not bad but it affects her health.'

'Is she as good-looking as you? Perhaps I can have her, too.'

'Don't say these things.'

And with that she smacks me, though not hard, and I know that I deserve it, for at that moment I would like all three of them.

Hitherto, though I have done the smacking, I have never let any woman strike me. Despite setting out to sample all that is on offer, I have shunned the many dominant females offering 'corrective services'. But to be hit by Mimi in this manner seems appropriate. I know at that moment that she will do it again in the future and that I will let her and I will enjoy it. Already she is unleashing a new side of my nature, one I have specifically avoided before now.

It brings to mind a silly quotation found over many glasses of port with a close friend in a university study: 'She hit me, but oh, so gently, it was almost a caress.'

I call her Scheherezade and wonder what kind of badness all this is supposed to be for the stories tell of a free spirit with a sense of humour.

I read an article about the role of eye contact when in love and realise that we are gazing into one another's eyes like lovers.

July opens with a perfect summer's day. I spend an hour with Mimi over lunch time, our bodies entwining as we toy with one another psychologically and physically as she delivers pleasure without parallel. Afterwards I rub shoulders with community transport providers at a country house on the edge of London, receiving congratulations on the annual report I have written for them.

As ever, I speculate about what they would think if they had seen how I had passed the previous hour, even though I display the outward forms of propriety.

The conference closes with a cocktail party from which I roll home, merry but not inebriated. H responds to my evident happiness by dressing in corset and suspenders and making love to me herself. Some days are just perfect.

In mid July, H and I go on holiday. We have no particular destination or intention as, over three weeks, we tour through the French Alps, Switzerland and Austria. Throughout the trip, I pine for Mimi and it is perhaps inevitable that I guide our meandering journey towards Eastern Europe. In Bratislava we wander around the old town.

Wanting and aching to talk about Mimi, I can at least mentally tease myself by straying towards dangerous ground where I can have Mimi playing in my mind. To H, as we walk around the pretty streets where I know that Casanova once trod, I declare the women to be quite simply beautiful. She agrees and we discuss why. I suggest that it is a one- or two-generation product of the transition from communism to capitalism.

'They grew up under the privations of communism, free of the obesity-inducing Western diet of junk food, which means they are slim and pretty. And now they are free, they flaunt themselves.'

'You mean they all dress like whores.'

'Perhaps, but you know I like that style. Tarts look good.'

'Quite. Left to you, I'd look like one,' she reminds me. 'But tarts don't age well.'

'Which is telling me not to run off with one.'

'You wouldn't like it in the long term.'

'I'd like to be back on Monday rather than Tuesday.'

'You're shortening my holiday by a day.'

'I've got one or two things I need to do. I need to drop into the LGA office to find out if I've still got my executive place.'

'I suppose so – if you must.'

I am not lying. I will pop into the Local Government Association and I do not know yet whether I have retained my position, but I am also being disingenuous for, despite a reasonably active sex life throughout the holiday, I am desperate to see Mimi. The extra day is of value because shortly after my return, she disappears back home for her own holiday.

The reunion is all I expect. Unfortunately she leaves the following week, so I will have seen her just twice in not far off two months and I am finding that being unable to see her literally hurts.

I inquire about seeing her off at the airport and/or meeting her on her return, but her boyfriend will be performing these functions. For the first time, this makes me begin properly to think of him. Hitherto he has been her *wanker*, an amusing backdrop to whom I can feel superior. But now I begin to be jealous, for he is the boyfriend of this marvellous creature. He presumably has free and on tap what I have to pay for and to which I am allowed only limited access.

'I come back the Tuesday. You may ring me.'

Which I do at four o'clock in the afternoon. She is short with me and tells me she is not well and I will not be able to see her until the following Tuesday.

On the Thursday, I ring the current Heathrow address on the off chance she might be working. She is.

That afternoon I present myself and surprise her.

'I never gave permission for you to see me today.'

'But when I found out you were working –'

'I am not well,' she snaps. 'I work today only because they ask me but I do not want to be here and I do not want to see you. I spent most of holiday ill and my mother treat me like child and I went to dentist because they cannot do good dentistry in this lousy country of yours and my teeth hurt.'

'I'm sorry, I –'

'And you ring me just as I meet my boyfriend at the airport and he want to know who is ringing me and that is difficult for me.'

I slink away like some naughty, whipped dog. Worse, I have a council meeting that night. I simply cannot face it. Instead I give my apologies, ring H, tell her I will be home that evening and would like a really nice meal and sex. She gracefully obliges – and I am grateful but the truth is that it is a pale imitation of what I want.

Sex with Mimi surpasses what anyone else is able to do for me – this from a woman who so humiliates me that she will not even accept my money to have sex with her. The cold reality is that I have gone to a brothel to see a woman I imagine I love and, though she will sell herself to other callers, all of whom she considers 'wankers', she simply sends me away to wait and pine and want.

I am certain most men would simply say, 'Fuck you, darling.' Why do I not do this, for I know I will turn up the following Tuesday all the more desperate for her? Have I no pride?

I arrange to see an old friend. We go so far back that to insult one another is impossible. We share the unvarnished truth about the other as we see it. He tells me that frankly I am being ridiculous getting steamed up over some stupid Russian tart when London is stuffed full of such women who would be grateful to have a clean, well-mannered, well-off English gentleman as a client. Moreover, to be jealous of her no doubt thuggish Serbian pimp is simply pathetic. He tells me I am allowing myself to be manipulated and controlled by my prick. He thinks I should have more sense and he quotes to me Lord Chesterfield on having a mistress: 'The expense damnable, the pleasure momentary and the position ridiculous.'

I can understand what he is saying but it has no emotional resonance. I know the meaning of the words but I simply do not relate to them. He tells me that I remain the pathetic, romantic idiot that I was at school and Oxford, that I have never grown up and have learned nothing, and that I am as bad at wooing and making myself loved as I ever was.

As I think that I tend to go for bitches and ask him why, he adds that I am about as effective with women as I am with selection committees. This linkage, established as we move from the second to the third bottle, is positively cruel.

For at that moment, my entire life feels like one long experience of being rejected – and I know all about rejection. I have added rejection by a whore in a brothel to a list which includes the women of Oxford – though I blame not myself but the gender ratio of seven or eight to one – the British public, selection committees and the electorate. It is much harder to become an MP than to be one.

* * *

I go to a seedy run-down hotel in the West Midlands.

After a twenty-minute wait, I am ushered into a shabby conference room occupied by 25 (mostly elderly) people and not a single smile between them: a condemned man could scarcely see grimmer countenances. I decide they need cheering up.

'Tony Blair dies and gets to the Pearly Gates. To his surprise, St Peter says, "Tony, it's up to you, you can come in here or go down there. And you've got twenty-four hours to decide. Come in, take a look around. Try down there if you like. Then come back and let me know your decision."

'So Tony goes into heaven and it's pretty much as you'd expect. Everybody is very good and worthy, standing around in long white robes, playing harps and singing hymns, but after a while Tony is bored.

'So he goes down there. The devil greets him enthusiastically and it's just one great party: fine wines, cordon bleu cooking, all his favourite luvvies being witty, entertaining and beautiful. Tony is entranced. Twenty-three hours later, he says apologetically to St Peter that he's going down there.

'But this time when he arrives, he finds bodies burning in the fiery furnace, others being tortured with much wailing and gnashing of teeth. He turns to the devil and says, "But it wasn't like this before!"

' "Ah," says the devil. "That was the manifesto." '

It won a wave of laughter and approval when I told several thousand people at the party conference. Here it barely raises a flicker. I carry on digging.

'The joke illustrates a fundamental truth: Blair is all mouth and no trousers. He does not deliver, he will not deliver and he cannot deliver.'

My mind disassociates itself as I think to myself, This is a complete waste of time. I don't like you and you don't like me . . .

I am right – they don't.

At an Essex selection committee, even the men wear white shoes.

'What makes you laugh?' they ask me.

'Irony.'

They don't like irony in Essex – or at least Conservatives don't!

At another selection, I am well liked, but lose anyway. The constituency chairman quietly tells H, 'Your husband is, of course, far and away the best but he's too like their former MP. They want one of their own, a local.'

I grow to hate the stupidity and inanity of Conservatives like the woman who asks, 'We've established that you can speak and that you can write but tell me, do you canvass?'

This question is so soul-destroyingly stupid that I am at a loss for words. 'No, of course not, I've been a Parliamentary candidate, a local councillor for many years and held every possible constituency position, but in all that time, I've never ever been on a doorstep.' But irony at the expense of one's selectors is not a virtue they appreciate.

When I am finally selected I break all the rules. I arrive twenty minutes late, an unforgivable sin.

'Look, I'm very sorry I'm late but it just goes to show how badly we need a proper dual carriageway from here to the motorway.'

The committee's laughter is spontaneous and I beam back.

'What do you know about us?' they ask.

I deliver an impromptu history lesson, reaching the arrival of the railway before they interrupt me: 'OK, we get the point, you clearly know an awful lot about the area.'

H doesn't want me to get it so, for the drinks party, she wears a miniskirt. 'They won't approve of a candidate's wife showing that much leg!' she says.

But they do or, at least, they don't disapprove sufficiently.

At the final showdown, the selectorate consists almost entirely of post-menopausal women – which makes the first question a nightmare.

'I'm the local HIV and AIDS co-ordinator. How would you vote on the lowering the age of consent for homosexuals to sixteen?'

'I would vote for it – for these reasons. First, I'm old enough to have gone to a traditional all-male English public school. We knew the guys who were homosexual. They weren't made that way by school, they were born that way. And American research shows particular gene patterns characterise gays and lesbians. If you look at the truly dreadful punishments imposed for buggery, then men have got to be mad or driven not to sleep with women. The state has no place in the bedroom.'

Sharp intakes of breath show the consternation in the room. Once again, I have blown it at the last hurdle.

And then the chairman comes out with a strange smile on his face. 'I am delighted to tell you, that we have decided to adopt you as our candidate.'

I am too shocked to reach for his outstretched hand. But it merely delays the inevitable. Electorates are as fickle and capricious as selection committees. It was Enoch Powell who famously said that all political careers end in failure. The higher you go, the greater the fall: if the electorate doesn't bring about your downfall, then one's own party will see to it.

At the 1997 general election I fail to win the seat.

SEVENTEEN

'I have condemned him only for being caught'

Back to another round of party conferences and again I am going to all three. I am pleased at the locations: Liberal Democrats and the Conservatives in Bournemouth, sandwiching the Labour party in Brighton and no Black-pool, thank goodness.

As I drive to Bournemouth in the Jaguar I have already taken a decision. For, though I was not able to identify with my old friend's words and walk away, I feel he is right in that Mimi is controlling me and the best way to protect myself is not to be faithful. By using the party conferences to continue my escapades, I feel I am retaining a measure of pride and independence. The alternative, confining my activities to Mimi and H, will merely replace one woman manipulating my desire for her with two!

Moreover, Mimi and I have discussed fidelity. She says, 'Any boyfriend of mine would not go to places like these. I would not allow it. I allow him to have other women occasionally on business trips when I am not around, but that is all.'

So, although she does not know it and I do not intend to draw my 'infidelity' to her attention, I am keeping to her rules as she set them out.

Besides, I am hoping to find the superb and delectable Tanya again.

I have booked my own hotel: it's slightly further out but the walk will do me good and it has a swimming pool and gym, which means I can keep my now much trimmer body the way I like it.

That is a source of pride. For by now I have shed and kept off over three stone. My father has told me that he hadn't liked to say but I had become fat and seedy. I point out that my motivation has been entirely sexual: good outcomes may arise from bad intentions and vice versa.

My first conference engagement is a private lunch with, hopefully, half a dozen Lib-Dem MPs. I say hopefully, but in fact I think we will be lucky to get half that number. They have been carefully invited but the replies were imprecise, which smells to me like multiple commitments and no-shows.

The lunch is in the Royal Bath Hotel, where the food is excellent with ample wine, champagne and a fine claret. In the event there are only three of us to consume it: myself, an aide and an MP who's about to retire. The result is a small, intimate lunch. The MP, who is good company, stays drinking champagne with me. When he goes, some time after three, I start talking to the waitress. She, it turns out, is a travelling American graduate going on to do a doctorate in art history at UCLA. I invite her to sit down and join me. She says she cannot, but she stands there for the best part of an hour as we discuss history, art and sex. I suggest most art comes from men because it is a form of display: 'look how fit and clever I am so come and have sex with me'. She says this is reductionist and finds it difficult to stomach but nonetheless stays as I seek to impress her with my learning.

When her floor manager comes along, I say, 'Look, she is just doing her job and excellently looking after a customer. If anybody is to blame here it's me for detaining her and, despite my offers, she will not accept a glass because she is supposed to be working.'

He smiles and she stays with me until I have emptied the bottle.

I have retained the number of Tanya's place of work, but when I ring am told that she left ages ago.

'Do you know where she is now?'

'No idea, love, but we've got a couple of very nice girls.'

'But I want Tanya.'

Instead I seek out a local paper, look through the small ads, take a walk and, by about six o'clock, am talking to a tall, slim, olive-skinned half South African, half Portuguese dressed in a corset and fishnet stockings. I run the two nationalities together and christen her Sappho, which instantly amuses her and gets us off on the right foot.

Being a working girl is an occupation which tends to leave even the most self-assured feeling somewhat vulnerable to their customers. Because I know this, I counter it by leaving the most immediate practical decisions to them.

Sappho offers a massage.

'That would be very nice, thank you.'

'Talc or oil.'

'Whichever you prefer.'

She uses oil and, because I am allowing her control, she genuinely seeks to give me the best time she can.

When we are about to have sex, she says, 'What position?'

'You choose.'

And she opts for what seems in my experience to be the working girl's position of choice, on top, again where she is in control.

And because she is in control, she does most of the work and makes it excellent. I ask about her hours and shifts and four hours, two receptions and an interesting conversation about community railways with a Liberal Democrat later – I am back having sex with Sappho a second time.

I explain that I am there this week and will be back the week after next. Across the six days I am in Bournemouth we see one another nine times – long enough to develop a relationship and come to like one another. She is married but separated. Her husband is an older man and very controlling; he's not violent or even aggressive but treats her more like a daughter than a wife. Whilst her parents look after her own daughter, she is travelling prior to going back to South Africa to set up a dance studio.

I tell her about H, my sons and Mimi.

'Do you love Mimi?'

'Yes, passionately.'

'So why are you here with me?'

'Because you are desirable too, and I cannot have her here and now, whereas I can have you and . . .'

She tells me I am more mixed-up than I think I am, that I must be searching for something but don't myself yet know what, and wishes me luck in my quest. It's a new perspective, for I have never thought of it in this way.

In Brighton, I have, amongst others, a student just two years older than my eldest son. It is eleven o'clock at night, we are naked and I am just about to enter her when my phone goes. It is my younger son from his public school. I talk to him briefly and then start laughing.

'That was your son, wasn't it?'

'Yes.'

'How old is he?'

'That one is fifteen, the elder is seventeen. A lot closer in age to you than to me.'

She laughs too.

At the end I kiss her hand like an old-fashioned courtier. 'A privilege and a pleasure,' I tell her, and tip her a tenner.

She responds by putting her arms around my neck (she is, as usual, slightly taller than me) and kissing me on the mouth.

Then I leave to meet up with my Labour council colleagues to drink and talk into the small hours.

Back for the Conservatives in Bournemouth, and I am to chair a fringe meeting. It is not particularly well attended; about twenty people turn up. I have not met my main speaker before, but he is good value and unlike many politicians genuinely seems to know what he is talking about.

I have just finished winding up and am having a glass of wine when my phone goes. The deputy headmistress at my son's school introduces herself.

My heart misses a beat.

'Have I picked a good time?'

'Well, yes and no, I am at the Conservative conference in Bournemouth and I've just finished chairing a meeting.'

She tells me the reason for her call.

'I'm afraid your son's been caught with smoking materials on him.'

'Oh!'

'We didn't actually catch him smoking.'

'So technically he hasn't committed an offence?'

'Well, clearly, he's not supposed to have the materials. Anyway, I would like you to come and collect him on Friday so we can discuss the matter. In the meantime, we are considering what disciplinary action is appropriate.'

'I will be there to pick him up on Friday.'

I am seriously concerned because I have a pretty shrewd idea what he has actually been up to.

That night I see Sappho for the last time. As I leave I say, 'You're lovely, I don't suppose you'll get to London but if you do please look me up.'

'I might pass through on my way back to South Africa.'

I give her my card. From her, too, I get an affectionate kiss on the lips.

I leave after breakfast the following day, take a leisurely drive to meet Mimi near Heathrow and am beginning to be fellated by her when my phone goes.

'I'd better answer that.'

It is the school again.

'I'm afraid it's more serious than we thought. It turns out that your son may have been smoking cannabis. We are suspending him for three days and you have to come here to collect him immediately.'

'Oh! Well . . . that's not terribly convenient. I'm right in the middle of, er, something. I'll try to be there at about five o'clock, depending upon the traffic.'

I end the call. Mimi asks what has happened.

'It's about my son, they've busted him for pot. I've got to go and pick him up.'

'That's your fault, you know.'

Damned in a single sentence with what I suspect will be the world's view. Mimi and I have discussed drugs. I wish to legalise them, quality-control them, tax them and turn them from a major cost to the state in an endless war that can never be won into a contributor to the exchequer. She believes I underestimate the extent to which this will encourage use.

'Do you want me to finish?'

'Of course! If only she could see me, the deputy head would think "like father, like son".'

'Ha! What if you had picture phone?'

'Something I never intend to have, it would reveal far too much.'

As usual, ten minutes later I am threshing in orgasmic ecstasy. She smacks me extra hard and says, '*That* is for your son.'

I know I deserve it and welcome it.

As I drive to his school, high Victorian grandeur and scenic sports pitches accompanied by appropriate modernisation, I know that I have to save him, not merely for his sake but because my self-respect is on the line. If I cannot save him, then I am not the person I think I am and I cannot look Mimi in the eyes again for, in a single sentence, she has made herself the voice of a censorious world, which does not understand the counter-intuitive logic of my beliefs.

I am interviewed by the deputy head before picking him up. She calls me 'Mr –' but I deliberately use her first name: an old trick but potentially marginally useful in the psychology of the relationship, for it gives me the upper hand. As I speak to her I am inwardly laughing at the idea of what she would think if she could have seen me when we had our telephone conversation earlier.

After a brief chat she turns to the matter in hand.

'We didn't find any actual drugs, only large rolling papers. As far as I can make out, and from what he tells me –'

'You can believe him, he is a very honest boy.'

'Yes, we think so too.'

'The evidence is circumstantial, then?'

'But he has admitted it, which counts in his favour, as he has been honest with us. So we are simply going to suspend him for three days – and give him a final warning.'

Saved!

When I see him, I check no one else is in earshot and say, 'Cunt!'

'I know. Sorry.'

'Why the hell didn't you dump the stuff?'

147

'I know, I should have done.'

As we travel back I explain.

'You do realise that I *don't* want you to take drugs.'

'Of course I do.'

'And you do realise that my belief in legalisation is not because I want anybody to take them but because I believe that people inevitably will and that taxation, quality control and a belief in individual freedom all make it the right option in a civilised society?'

I lecture him to the effect that as illegal drugs are a market and price is a function of supply, government action to restrict it is self-defeating because it stimulates what it tries to stop. Every destroyed cannabis plant or poppy field, every customs seizure or taking out of dealers actually brings new people into the market. Attempts to stop it are a grotesque and costly waste of time, money and effort. More perverse incentives created by posturing politicians with whom I less and less identify or even like, though I am one myself!

But as I finish I know something else that he also knows. I do not consider his behaviour wrong. I have condemned him only for being caught.

Later, H is concerned and understanding, but then she took pot throughout her student years and only gave up because I asked her to in the context of my political aspirations.

That weekend, I see my father and tell him H's reaction but also Mimi's opinion on the matter – that my son's behaviour is my fault for being so liberal. He says, 'I wasn't going to say it but since she has, that's rather my own view.'

I reflect on the simple proposition that I do not consider my current behaviour or my son's wrong. Indeed, the flouting of conventional thinking, the breaking of what I think of as bourgeois values, are both a source of amusement and part of the pleasure. In that sense Mimi and my father are right: I do not condemn, I condone and they know it. But, crucially, it is not possible for me to think otherwise and I despise the hypocrisy of political classes the world over who do one thing but say another.

We keep it all from my mother for she would not like this, she would worry and blame me – probably volubly. But then, we also keep from her that I am consorting with prostitutes.

EIGHTEEN

'I am becoming more submissive and she more dominant'

'I saved him,' I tell Mimi.

'I knew you would. You English upper-middle class with your children, you spoil them. When I get pregnant, my parents said I had to sort it out. I had to find money for abortion. I had to work with horses in what are they called, yes, stables. I had to save myself and learn lesson. He will do it again.'

'We've talked about it and I trust him.'

'You think he will tell you truth?'

'Yes, because he knows he can.'

'I do not think so. You are, what's word, naïve. You trust too much.'

'Only when I think I can. I trust you, for instance.'

By this stage, she is playing with me.

'How you know? What if one day I decide to bite it off?'

'That wouldn't be in your interests.'

'Bullshit. I might decide to do it.'

But what she actually does is bring me to the usual stupendous, long-lived orgasm.

After sex she smacks me.

'I always do that after, because you might enjoy it too much before.'

But I suspect she actually knows that the not very powerful, open-handed hits she gives me as I thresh without self-control in an extended orgasm only add to the sheer pleasure.

Progressively, she is smacking me more and I like it. I feel I am becoming more submissive and she more dominant, her comments more provoking and challenging, and I like that too. I wonder if I am looking to be punished for my own behaviour even though I believe that I am doing nothing wrong.

As I dress, she has clearly been contemplating my more practical vulnerabilities.

'What's your favourite paper?'

'*The Economist.*'

'No, I mean proper paper.'

'*The Sunday Times.*'

'How would you like to be in it, big piece?'

'Depends upon the piece.'

'Two pages, all about you and what you do with me and your wife, your son's school drugs, very nice that one, and all the rest of it. What if I splash you all across your favourite paper?'

'I know exactly what I'd say. They'd have photographs of you and my wife, I'd make sure they had, and you would both look gorgeous and then I'd simply say, "Look at them, what man wouldn't, given the chance, so how can you blame me?"'

'And you think you'd get away with that?'

'Depends what you mean by get away with it. Most politicians create problems for themselves because they can't face up to the truth, so they get themselves in trouble by lying. I wouldn't lie because I have done and am doing nothing of which I am ashamed. Actually for a man, if this kind of story is handled in a certain way, he can emerge as a bit of an old dog, interestingly. It's a compliment for a man but a terrible insult for a woman. One of the differences between us is that *you* think what you do is wrong. *I* don't. What would happen is that you would be splashed across the piece as well – I would ensure that – and then you would be investigated.'

'They'd have nothing on me. I am good at these things. I am legal.'

'I know you are, sweetheart, and so am I, but it would at best all become terribly inconvenient for you. I know how to handle these things and I have carefully ensured that our relationship carries an equal risk for both of us; I have something on you and you have something on me. It's a sound principle, ideally to be applied in all relationships.'

To mark our six-month anniversary, I give her a Karen Millen dress. The next time I see her, I ask if she likes it. She says she does, and I also realise something else. At no stage, despite all the many presents I have given her, can I ever recall her saying 'thank you'.

I see there's a public debate coming up on prostitution. I tell Mimi that I intend to go.

'I bet they don't have working girl among speakers.'

'I'm sure you're right.'

'You should arrange for me to be speaker. I will know more about it than any of them and I will correct rubbish that they will talk about business of which they know nothing.'

'I would love to, but somehow I don't think it in either of our interests to make this happen, though I am certain you would do it very well, could teach them a lot and would be an absolute wow.'

'Perhaps you will ask question?'

'Somehow I don't think so, for where and how did I acquire my knowledge?'

As I expect, there are many more women than men and a clear divide in opinion between those who simply wish to ban prostitution and those who count it as inevitable and therefore something to be managed whilst protecting the sex workers.

Only one speaker from the SW5 project (ironically in the context of male and transgender prostitutes for whom the organisation provides advice) makes the point that sex workers are not all victims trying to give it up but that prostitution can be a lifestyle choice.

He is aware that this view is verging upon heresy and he apologises for the opinion even though he says he knows it to be the case amongst many working girls as well. His courage is evident from the speech of a Labour MP, who says that in her opinion the goal must be to end prostitution. I reflect on how I would like to be able to take her to meet Mimi or Tanya or many of my other sexual partners, but her messianic tone seems to me to indicate that her mind is made up. She appears to view all prostitutes as victims to whom she is superior; none can be equals whose choices she should respect. It is the old socialist logic of 'I know what is good for you and what you *think* you want merely indicates you are not fit to decide.'

Fortunately the minister present gives no commitments.

As we have pre-arranged, because it appeals to both our senses of humour, I slide quietly out just before the close, pick up two copies of the take-away pack, one for me and one for Mimi, and within an hour am enjoying the very experience which has been the subject of the debate.

I reflect that the Labour MP would, without doubt, have been truly appalled.

NINETEEN

'You can screw some Eastern Europeans on their home ground'

It is New Year's Eve. Late in the morning I take a call from an old friend, we'll call him Bruce, who works for the asset management arm of a major merchant bank (or rather, did). That is the purpose of the call. He has been made redundant and wants to talk to me.

We arrange to meet in a wine bar.

Over a couple of bottles of wine, he divulges his thoughts. I have to pace my drinking. What he is saying is sufficiently serious that I need to take it in. Also I have three parties tonight, though I think I will only make two. Unfortunately it is Freddy's I will miss, which is a shame, but unavoidable in terms of logistics. At the final one I am meeting H and she will be furious with me if I turn up completely pissed.

Bruce is 31, unmarried, nearly six foot, slim and I suppose good-looking in a large-nosed, big-eyed, sandy-haired way. I say good-looking because his sexual success is vast and I'm never quite sure why. He has never struck me as particularly attractive but I have watched women swoon before him after just five minutes in his company. In some ways it irritates me and I am jealous. My father says such men emit hidden pheromones to which women subconsciously respond. I will probably never know if my father is right about the pheromones but if he is, and people like Bruce do, then my lifetime's success with women tells me that I do not.

'. . . so what I am suggesting is that we do something together focused on Eastern Europe, particularly the now independent former Soviet states.'

He suggests some business ventures we could investigate.

I listen and then ask, 'Where?'

He lists some Eastern European cities and then pauses for dramatic effect. 'You can screw some Eastern Europeans on their home ground.'

Bruce clearly knows my reputation.

'So we can have some fun and try to make some money. What do you think?'

'Well, I'm flattered', I reply, 'but why me?'

'Because you're a dirty bastard and I think we'll get on. But also you actually know more about running a business than I do, you have gravitas which I lack, your contacts are bloody good and I need someone calmer than me who will fucking well tell me to stop when I need to. So, what d'you say, mate?'

'I'll need to think about it.'

'Just take a few days' leave and come with me on a reconnaissance trip. Do some research, check out the local opportunities.' He sighs, patiently. 'It's a no-brainer really, mate.'

'I'll have to talk it over with H.'

But I know that I am going to accept; there are too many Eastern European women that I have not yet had, too many shady bars I want to drink in, too much of the darkness I want to sample to pass up such an offer. The politics in which I have passed so much of my adulthood has not offered the expected rewards and pleasures. Notwithstanding all I have already done, I need to seek more of life and I feel that can be found in the newly emerging post-communist world, what Bruce has called the 21st-century Wild West. I think I can survive and, if I can, it is an experience I have to have whatever the consequences.

Inevitably, all of this makes me focus back on the Russian I want more than any other right now. Thus, when Bruce and I part at about five o'clock I am desperate for Mimi, but she's told me she's unavailable over the New Year. I won't be able to see her until the 4th. So I send her a text: 'Completely utterly totally love you happy new year'.

'It did *not* help!'

'What?'

'Your stupid text! It did not help.'

'Why not? It was supposed to make you feel good.'

She grunts. 'I had *shit* New Year, ended up drinking bottle of champagne by myself.'

I think of the one I gave her on the 28th.

'So what happened?'

'My *wanker* boyfriend again. We have row about parking tickets. He owes hundreds of pounds and he doesn't pay them, so I tell him to pay or he will end up being prosecuted, so he says he hasn't got money and asks me for it, so I tell him he is stupid to get them and to pay his own *fucking* tickets. I need money for deposit on flat as I need to move. He storms out to see friends but he was supposed to come back over about ten so we could be together but he does not come so I send text telling him to *fuck off*. So I open bottle of champagne by myself and *fucking* drink it.'

As I listen to this, his daft behaviour assuages my pangs of jealousy.

'Have you made up?'

She grunts again. 'I've seen him but I am bad so I end up throwing cups at him. However, I think a little and I throw cups which I do not like so they do not matter. I will get new ones when I move.'

As ever, she does not seem to me the bad or fallen woman she seems to think herself. But then, as I am discovering, Eastern European women seem to have some very traditional values, prostitutes especially so.

'You've found a new flat?'

'Yes and no. I've found flat but I have problem.'

I raise my eyebrows quizzically and she looks down at me for she is occupying a rattan chair dressed only in expensive, flowery, lacy bra and thong whilst I am kneeling naked between her legs as if in worship.

'I do not like to do this. Is difficult for me,' she grumbles. 'I hate asking for money but . . . I need deposit on flat.'

'How much?'

'Two thousand pounds.'

At this point I think of what my friend said about me allowing myself to be controlled by my prick and know that he, like most men, would take me for a fool in what I am about to do. Perhaps I am! But the fact is I know this woman by now. She is proud. She worries about her reputation and hates the word 'prostitute'. Part of what she earns goes to her family back home. Far from condemning her, I admire her bravery and I genuinely think it takes courage to ask me. Still kneeling before her, I say, 'And you know perfectly well I am going to give it to you.'

'Yes, I know this thing. But it is not easy for me.'

'I've brought the money.'

'Good.'

But there's a catch.

'I'm afraid it's a cheque.'

I get out my cheque book and a pen and then stop and look into her eyes. 'In order to write you a cheque, I need a name, your real name or at least the name you use for your account.'

She laughs nervously. 'Give me pen and I will write it for you.'

But even then she hesitates for she hates anything about her to be traceable. I wait, smiling.

'I cannot give you the money without a name.'

Eventually she writes it on a piece of paper. I take it from her, make out the cheque, hand it over and begin to fold the paper with her writing on it.

'Hey, give it back to me.'

'No,' I say, half smiling, half laughing at her. She goes to snatch it from me and I pull away whilst trying to pronounce it. She corrects me whilst still trying to grab the paper.

'I'm keeping that, I'm afraid, Ms –'

And I call her by her real name for the first time and then ask, 'So what is your first name?'

'You always ask so many questions.'

'It's entirely reasonable to want to know your name, and whilst we are about it, I also want to know your address, the one I'm giving you two thousand pounds as a deposit for.'

'You are too curious and what did curiosity do?'

She answers her own question. 'It kill cat.'

But when I leave I do know her name and address and have been asked by her if I can run a check on the ownership of the place she is about to occupy.

This pleases me for I feel I am winning her confidence. It makes me feel useful to her and that brings happiness, for in my experience most men want to feel useful to the woman or women they love.

A couple of days later, I am sitting in a wine bar with a friend who works for a trade association when my mobile rings.

'It is Mimi, your cheque has problem.'

'I don't see why it should, I can assure you there are more than enough funds in the account.'

'I visit my bank and they will not give me money.'

'These things always take a couple of days to clear.'

'Can you check with your bank?'

I do so, then ring her back to tell her that the money has left my account.

My companion inquires, 'What was all that about? She seems desperate for the money.'

When I explain, he comments, 'Presumably the boyfriend is her pimp.'

'I've been wondering about that,' I say. 'Some parts of their relationship seem like that, others don't. If he is, he's not very good at it for he doesn't seem to have any money. He's certainly not big-time Russian mafia or anything like that because they wouldn't piss around with me in this way. Truth to tell, I'm not really sure.'

After he leaves, I contemplate my feelings about Mimi's man who is, I suspect, going to become increasingly important in my life. She was bound to have a man for you are not someone like Mimi without one. The line between pimp and boyfriend is not clear-cut: at what point does one become the other? I genuinely do not care; it seems to me it may be a distinction without a difference. And even if he is her pimp, what difference should it make to my behaviour? I will still behave in the same way: responding with both alacrity and efficiency to the many demands that are going to be made of me by the woman with whom I have fallen in love.

*   *   *

Bruce rings to tell me we are flying to Riga, leaving late afternoon. I arrange my diary. A meeting in the morning, followed by a visit to Mimi and then on to Heathrow.

I give Mimi a stuffed Siberian tiger as a present. It fills my briefcase and during my meeting I wonder what my colleagues would think if they knew the case's contents. It necessitates careful opening to extract papers as I do not wish to have to make up some story to explain it away.

I preface giving it to her by saying, 'I don't normally do this kind of thing, but it was so appropriate: it comes from Russia and – just like you – it's exotic, beautiful and fierce yet also soft and cuddly and gorgeous all at the same time.'

To my pleasure, her eyes light up; my silly present is a success.

I tell her where I am going and why. She issues me a stark warning: 'Be careful, you think you can play at doing business over there, but much is run by Russian mafia. I think you must go carefully and remember your English ways are not theirs. You talk lots and give much away. They want deals and action and will be upset if you do not deliver on promises.'

She presents her face for me to kiss her goodbye in a manner which feels wifely, and when her last words are 'Come back safe', I feel loved.

We are met amidst the snows of Riga airport by Keith, who is slim and good-looking in a dissolute sort of way, with blond hair. He makes life simple for he chauffeurs us around, lets us stay in his apartment and knows the ways of the city, which immediately comes across as busy, modern and, at least superficially, Westernised, much more so than I perhaps expect.

We drop off our baggage. The flat is in a nondescript seven-storey block which could be anywhere in Europe. It looks like it dates from the 1950s but is large and well appointed with the kind of outsized, real wooden furniture that is not much seen in the UK.

I ask advice on what I should wear.

Bruce simply says, 'Up to you, mate,' but Keith understands the question.

'You want to look as though you've got money but not like a Western wanker, so no tie – that marks you out as a typical Western businessman – but keep the expensive suit on, wear a plain sweater underneath and the expensive overcoat, not the anorak, over the top.'

Thus suitably attired and less than an hour after arriving, we are out on the piss. They take me on a whistle-stop tour of the nightlife, which becomes a hazy profusion of bars, clubs and lap-dancing joints. All I have is impressions of beautiful women in dark seedy dives not dissimilar to those I have frequented in London, with the same sense of décor, all dark colours, velvets and shadow-throwing up-lighting.

The heavies, however, are much more menacing than London's penguins. With crew cuts and large, muscular bodies dressed in black from head to toe, they exude a constant air of barely suppressed violence, a pervasive sense of menace, exacerbated by the way they square up to the visible inebriation of many of the customers. Later I will see them in action. It is not pretty and I will wonder to what extent this is how Mimi's boyfriend is.

My favourite establishment is barely two minutes from the flat. It includes a large nightclub, with a crowd of gyrating bodies, mostly attractive females. Of the people standing around, most are men who are eyeing up the talent but are simply unworthy of the beauty on display.

Keith comments on this: 'Yeah, all the women are stunning, and all the men are complete pisshead wankers! Never know how all blokes can be a lower form of life than all birds. You wouldn't have thought it genetically possible, would you?'

The place also includes a large lap-dancing bar where the women are even more beautiful.

'They don't deal in categories like we do,' he explains. 'Same ownership and blokes here switch from one to the other. The bosses use it as their VIP area. If you're important enough, I reckon the women are on the house.'

'As an arrangement, it's entirely logical, but I suspect that in London the licensing complications would be horrendous,' I observe, whilst thinking that, right now, a woman on the house is exactly what I want.'

I approach the door man and make some inquiries. He tells me he'll organise a car with three women inside for me to choose from, at which point I'll agree a price. Bruce and Keith have agreed, out of kindness, to let me have the bedroom back at the flat.

'Go on.'

It works just as the door man says and some minutes later I enter the flat arm in arm with a pretty dark-haired, snub-nosed Russian.

Once she has phoned her minder to confirm her safe arrival, turned down the drink I have offered and used the bathroom, we try to talk. Success is limited but it establishes human contact. She then sets to work doing everything. She undresses me, puts me in the bed, sits down beside me flaunting her body as she slowly removes her own clothing to unveil it, gently pushes me across to give herself room to climb in beside me, and then begins passionately French-kissing me, her tongue darting in and around my mouth. The mouth has soon descended to my crotch where I notice that her technique is more or less identical to Mimi's.

I briefly wonder whether they have both been to the same Eastern European prostitutes' training school, as I imagine that under practical communist efficiency such things might really have existed. Then oral sex gives way to penetration, she remaining the active party, I the passive.

It becomes clear that, whilst erection is no problem, my orgasm will have to be postponed. The combined effects of drink, tiredness and the fact I have been with Mimi earlier in the day, are finally catching up with me.

She takes this as a challenge and we begin to alternate masturbation, penetration and fellatio performed in sequence like the steps of a dance. I fondle promiscuously and my fingers penetrate her bottom without complaint. After a time, she tells me I must pay more and I realise that Bruce and Keith have all the money.

Saying, 'Hang on a mo,' I seek them out on fold-up beds in a darkened sitting room to be given a combination of lats and dollars and the comment that I am 'a bloody noisy cunt'. When I return she is just finishing a conversation which I take to be with her minder explaining the situation.

We recommence and orgasm swiftly follows – but it is hers not mine as she moans and writhes beneath me. I feel it must be real for a fake orgasm at that point makes little sense. She does not attempt, however, to force my withdrawal and, as our combined sweat lubricates the movement of our bodies against one another, I finally follow with much loud grunting and groaning. I am entirely satisfied and think she has earned every cent.

I lie there in a post-orgasmic glow as she goes to the bathroom, cleans herself, comes back, cleans me, and then dresses, all the time with smiles and laughter playing about her face as if the whole experience has been one long, entertaining joke. She calls her minder and I am soon seeing her out, though she asks for two of my business cards, the second of which she hands back to me having written her name and phone number on it.

I hear a voice say, 'Thank fucking Christ for that, now perhaps we can get some bloody sleep!'

At eleven o'clock the next day, Bruce has arranged for us to drink green tea with some Latvian businessmen to discuss the need for investment and how it can be attracted from the West.

In the event, I find myself talking about UK Treasury rules which preclude local government bond issues. I draw from personal experience of sitting on committees where I have sat alongside Conservative MPs.

Later I find myself reflecting on how rare the capacity for the truth is in politics. I get more honesty from the whores and their associates who are now my chosen company than I do from the politicians who, with one or two notable exceptions, I increasingly find self-satisfied and self-serving. They do not necessarily start out that way but the process makes them so. Tell the truth, complex and difficult as it usually is, and you are hounded by public opinion.

The meeting lasts nearly three hours and is followed by a long, late lunch at which Bruce and Keith comment that my performance of the morning is as remarkable as my performance of the night before. I think this is a compliment.

Lunch slides effortlessly into drinks and we are soon in a lap-dancing club where I am talking to a tall Russian blonde and a shorter Latvian brunette who tells us in rather good English that she is studying public administration at Riga University. To the blonde's disgust (for she knows that she is the one I fancy more) I take the brunette to the booth. There in privacy I sit her down and explain that I want her number because I may need a briefing on Latvian local government finance structures.

If she is surprised – and working girls rarely admit to it, having seen most things – she does not show it. Nevertheless, it must be one of the more bizarre requests she has received from a customer. Again, passing over two of my cards procures her number and gives her mine. She then tells me that she would like to dance for me anyway, as that is what I am paying for. I am beginning to be truly impressed by the professionalism of the women of Latvia.

The evening ends in a karaoke bar like none I have ever seen. The building is like something out of sixteenth-century England, heavy timber with beams and old-fashioned carpentry. The place is awash with ash, beer dregs and a clientele many of whom are like a Bruegel painting come to life.

In the wrong mood it would probably be hell, but tonight it is actually just funny. Latvian karaoke is simply surreal.

However, at least half the available songs are in English and Bruce decides it is time for him to become Elvis. He is actually very good, and acquires a Latvian fan club, some of whom sing along, and we end up in conversation with a group of Riga University students.

As I begin to converse with one, a drunk starts to proposition her and will not be put off. I go up to the door man and inform him of the situation. A couple of minutes later two black-attired legalised thugs appear, none too gently seize the man's arms and drag him away. He will literally be thrown out.

My companion tells me her name is Sofia and we begin to talk. She is studying philosophy and history and my knowledge impresses her. 'You are *only* Englishman I ever come across who know these things!'

Mimi said something very similar. Eastern European women seem to appreciate a good education more than their British counterparts, probably because Eastern European women are in turn better educated: many are graduates from education systems where far smaller numbers go to university.

Nearly two hours later, I have bought several rounds of drinks for the whole party and we have moved on to Hegel. I make the point that his dialectic always makes the oppressed and discontented the engine of change. 'Because the rich are content, they oppose change. Thus it is the underdog – thieves, prostitutes, the poor, the people Christ actually hung out with – who determine the future.'

In response, she leans across to me and slurring slightly says, 'You good man, I come back apartment with you.'

'Oh,' I say. 'That would be extremely nice.'

And a long-held Oxford University dream is realised at that moment. Camilla and Arabella and many others are compensated for. My learning has allowed me to talk my way between her legs.

'I get bag and coat. We go.'

She goes off whilst I ask Bruce and Keith whether they are ready to leave; they are.

As I watch Sofia return, she is accosted by a crew-cut young man with a filthy look on his face. Earnest conversation takes place. When she reaches me, her smile is gone. 'I have talk him. I back five minutes.'

Keith says quietly in my ear, 'Trouble and Russian, probably boyfriend rather than pimp but he still doesn't want a Westerner screwing his bird. You need to watch it and we may have to get the fuck out of here.'

'Bugger.'

She comes back to me. 'You good, nice man, I like sleep with you but – sorry! Not possible.'

She slips a piece of paper in my hand, kisses me and turns away.

'Tough luck, mate,' says Bruce, and they each take a shoulder and march me out before I can do or say anything stupid.

As I notice that the paper bears a mobile number, they push me in a taxi and Keith gives me some advice. 'This place has some very nasty and very jealous people in it that you really don't want to know.'

I sleep alone.

TWENTY

'I see Mimi punishing someone, beating them with birch rods'

By Heathrow's baggage carousels I change SIM cards, for I have acquired a Latvian telephone identity.

Within minutes, a text envelope appears. 'Hi, its Mimi. Can you call me back i need your advice and its emergency.'

Feeling useful and therefore loved, I ring her straight away.

'I'm at Heathrow. You wanted me.'

'Can landlord keep thousand pounds deposit?'

'Only if it's to cover damage, why?'

'I've been stupid. My landlord is being difficult so I find new flat and pay deposit. Then I talk to my landlord and we solve problem so I go and ask for my deposit back from other flat and they will not give it, say it cover first month's rent.'

'I'm certain they can't do that unless you signed something to that effect. Did you sign anything?'

'Yes, I stupid so I did.'

'Do you have a copy of it?'

'No, they did not give me it and I did not ask.'

I sigh. 'That was a bit daft. Where are you now?'

'Usual place, you come and see me?'

So, rather than going home, I visit Mimi en route and give her some money to sort out her troubles.

I phone my lawyer to check on the legal position and am soon sitting on the sofa with her and the maid talking through the problem and telling her what to do, which is basically to go back in person, inform them that they have no right to keep the money and that failure to pay it will result in legal action with a claim for costs.

'Will you come with me?'

'If you want me to, yes.'

And, again, I feel useful, and therefore wanted and loved. If my responses seem unbelievable – how can I allow myself to be used in this way whilst paying her for sex – then that feeling is almost certainly the key. At least my relationship with Mimi guarantees that she always gives me great sex. This is not something that has come reliably from other women in my life. Ultimately that is probably why I prefer to pay. The outcome is guaranteed. Remove the cash nexus and you remove that certainty.

Her problems attended to, if not solved, she calms down and devotes herself to my pleasure. Strangely, even as this most lovely of women gives me the most fantastic of blow jobs, I find myself not entirely here, but fantasising.

In my mind I see Mimi punishing someone, beating them with birch rods. At first, it is the Russian male, then it turns to Sofia, though even in my fantasy I decide that she does not deserve this so it switches to Angela. I imagine Angela as a schoolgirl, with Mimi as her governess beating her in front of me. Angela is bent over a trestle or an old-fashioned sloped wooden school desk with Mimi first smacking then birching her. I inspect and feel her handiwork. Mimi then makes Angela stand in the corner, her abused bottom on display, whilst Mimi gives me the very blow job she now is.

Of course afterwards, she strikes me, but not hard and only to my joy.

Late the following morning, shortly before I leave to join her, I get a text: 'I see him and he keep one week deposit so I lose £200, next time I will be more clever.'

When I next see her she says to me, 'My landlord have problem which is also my problem, you might be able to help?'

'Go on.'

'Is stupid inspectors. He has been doing up block and now they say he must change things he has already done because these things do not comply with regulations and the flat on which they do this is the flat he plans for me and he ask if I knew anybody who could help him. And I said "maybe" and thought of you.'

'You'd better bring me the paperwork.'

'Ha, I have it here.'

What she produces is a letter from the council about failure to comply with the terms of the planning consent for a listed building. There are half a dozen items.

'Can you help?'

'Yes, it's exactly the kind of thing I've done as a councillor. You'd better arrange for us to meet, but you need to understand that I am involving myself in all of this only because it's you. And I want you there at the meeting.'

'Do I have to be?'

'I'm doing it for you, because I love you, not for him. And I want to see you as part of this.'

'But I do not want you to meet my boyfriend, he must not see you. So we go for drink round corner and then I take you in and I make sure my boyfriend is not there, but his friends may see us so you must not do anything with me.'

'That's fine. And since you mention it, our relationship has long since ceased to be just about sex. If I came to you just for sex, I could get it more easily and cheaply elsewhere. You know I love you.'

She avoids my gaze.

'Maybe, we see. One more thing, my landlord he is not House of Commons, he is ordinary man so do not do what you always do and use long, complicated words. Keep it simple so he understands.'

This is all too reminiscent of what H and the proverbial person from Conservative Central Office have been telling me for years:

'You're too complicated, you lose people and threaten them rather than making them feel comfortable . . .'

'Don't use such long words and complex ideas: it may be right but this is not about the truth, you're wooing people . . .' and so on.

Freddy once summed it up over a second bottle of wine. Our business dealt with, I was explaining to him the problem of candidate interview-itis. 'It's getting to me, you know,' I complained.

'Go on, what is? What is interview-itis, as you call it?'

'It's like being on a constant roller coaster of heightened emotion. I apply for a seat, with no great expectation because I know there will be loads of applicants. The letter arrives. Have I or haven't I got an interview? If I haven't I'm fed up but if the answer's yes, the roller coaster continues. Have I got through the first interview – and the second – in a game where to be anything other than first is to be nowhere? It's all so bloody frustrating.'

'How's H taking it?'

'Oh, outwardly she's great as usual, but actually she's getting pissed off. She's already done nearly a dozen interviews herself. She has to pretend that it's the place she wants to live most in all the world – wherever it is. She has to laugh at jokes she's heard a dozen times and give the same adoring look – we call it the Hillary Clinton – to words she knows by heart.'

'You confuse them. They don't understand that you can be both dry as a bone economically and socially liberal – and that you're the one who's logical and consistent. You're too clever for them. And H supports this with a smart, even glamorous, image. To select the two of you the party has to be confident and it isn't. There's a phrase used in the City: "lean towards the order". Do you know what that means?'

'No.'

Freddy gives me one of his disdainful looks.

'It's a politer way of saying, "Fuck you, me first".'

'I see.'

Later, I have a conversation with a Tory who tells me how he came to be selected. 'If I'm honest with you, I got there as a fantasy object. The chairman, who was of course a middle-aged woman, told me that they chose me over the others because the elderly female members – which is most of 'em – liked my bum!'

So now, at precisely 6 p.m. as arranged, I get to see where Mimi lives: a typical large Edwardian terraced house divided into flats. I phone her just before I arrive and she comes down to take me in. Her landlord's greeting is effusive, but with him is a wiry man, probably in his thirties, with a weather-beaten face, wearing a black donkey jacket and an incongruous woollen hat. Who wears such a hat indoors?

He is introduced as the landlord's manager. That'll be a question for Mimi when we finish: who or what is he?

Her landlord has the Mediterranean sense of hospitality so the meeting is conducted with coffee and brandy. I try to perform as instructed, staying simple and to the point. The case is relatively straightforward. The building is listed and he has a planning consent that he has failed to follow to the letter, in large part because the pettifogging detail is ridiculous – they have to renovate the building exactly as it was when listed, they are not even allowed to restore it back to the Edwardian original.

An hour or so later, I have drafted a letter of response. This is more difficult than it sounds for they wish to convey their irritation at the absurdity of the regulations whereas my letter is co-operative, explaining that they will immediately begin to comply with what is easy and cheap to do and asking for a meeting about more serious, expensive breaches.

I explain the tactics. 'This gives the officials a result which you can live with and allows them to report success to their bosses. You clearly don't want the meeting and if they forget about it, that's great. If it happens, we'll make sure it takes time to arrange. If it does happen, I'll help you with it. We'll argue that, as you've taken out what was there, and there's no real record of what was there, who can possibly know!'

Afterwards Mimi and I go to a pub around the corner and I realise this is the very first time we have had a drink together. She has a Smirnoff® Ice, the red not the black, which seems appropriate enough, and pulls away when I try to hold her hand.

'Not in public, my boyfriend have lots of friends round here who know me and tell him. You must be more careful. He is jealous guy.'

'And what about that manager?'

'Oh, he friend of my boyfriend and how I come to be there. He suggest flat in first place.'

'So he will report back on me?'

'Maybe.'

'Look, can I ask you something? I've been meaning to for ages. You are clever and beautiful. There must have been someone else, what happened, why are you in this position?'

'So many questions . . .'

'I'm curious about everything about you.'

'And curiosity –'

' "Kill cat", I know, but . . .'

'I was not telling truth when I told you about my holiday last year. I did see my family but I did not go to Moscow, my family not from there, they are from –'

And I learn for the first time about her real background. I have enough knowledge to picture the post-communist middle-class poverty which is the birthright she seeks to escape, and where she helps to fund the family left behind.

She, meanwhile, adds to my knowledge: 'It is not like here. I have this friend, she have rich boyfriend but he gambles. One night he gambles away everything, money, car, house, till all he have left was her. Then he offer her for one last throw; he loses again. That's kind of place I come from and I have to leave. I think over here I look for millionaire but . . .'

'It's not that easy?'

'I have couple of girlfriends who marry very rich men. But me, I feel sorry for men. These girls they do exactly what they want and men have very hard time of it but I do not want these things at price they pay because most men drink too much or gamble; men are *wankers*.'

We sit silently for a moment. My mind is uneasy. I do not know how things will ever resolve, where the happy ending is, for her and for me. At the same time, she is slowly taking me into her confidence. For a prostitute, men are generally to be used but not trusted. This gradual evolution of mutual trust and confidence, her sharing of her life and past with me, is central to my ever-growing belief that she does love me, at least as much as she will ever love any man.

As we part, I wonder whether the woman who ended up as the stake in a gamble was not a friend but her. It would help account for her low opinion of men. But there are certain questions even I do not wish to ask.

Confronting people with their past can be a difficult and dangerous place to go, for we all reinvent ourselves to meet our own requirements. The more dubious our past, the greater the reinvention – and we really do not thank those who point out that it was not always so. It is something both politicians and working girls have in common: a professional requirement to sanitise, to dissemble.

At subsequent sessions with Mimi, I learn that my tactics have succeeded on her landlord's behalf. Still she never seems to say thank you.

I also learn that her boyfriend has given her a dog.

'What sort of dog you think I have?'

'I don't know.'

'Guess.'

'Well, not something soft and fluffy, something fierce.'

'You understand. I have pit bull. Others are terrified of him but I discipline him and he do what I say. He knows if people are afraid of him and he can make them frightened, but I control him. My girlfriend come round. She sits down on couch. I go out to make us coffee. I hear her call. When I come back, it is very funny. There is girlfriend squashed in corner of room with him growling at her. I tell him he is bad dog and he immediately stops. I do not beat him, I do not need to, I rule him, he knows I'm his mistress, his boss.'

'I think I identify!' I reply.

TWENTY-ONE

'I don't know what normal is any more'

B ruce proposes we go to Vilnius in Lithuania and then on to Minsk in Belarus.

I arrange for Mimi to meet Bruce, as I am interested to see how Mimi and Bruce get on. Mimi's commitments and needs dictate the venue, which is as deliberately anonymous as possible – the bar of one of London's great railway termini. She remains fearful of the prying eyes of her boyfriend's associates.

As we men arrive first, I buy us a Shiraz and Bruce is well into his second glass when Mimi turns up fifteen minutes late, looking both gorgeous and professional in a tightly cut black trouser suit beneath which I glimpse a sexy, lacy blouse. I rise and she presents her cheeks for kissing. One of the aspects of Eastern European women, whether working girls or not, is that they appreciate and expect the courtesies of a gentleman. They dislike yobbery.

She sits next to me and opposite him. I briefly take her hand under the table as conversation rapidly turns to the trials and tribulations of doing business in the territories of the former Soviet Union. Whereas I as yet have little to say, Bruce has very clear views.

'Nah, it's no different from doing business anywhere else.'

Mimi does not agree. 'I do not think so. I know way Russian mind works. It is not like Western mind. In West, especially in UK, is all talk, talk, talk and nothing happens for ages. You don't even start talking business until dessert. In former Soviet Union, is very direct, they want to see contract and sign. After that, they expect things to happen quickly.'

'Not true at all. Russian bureaucracy is a byword for the fact that nobody can take a decision.'

'You do not know what you talk about, I know these things, officials it maybe so, but in business is different, Russians sign deals very fast and expect things to happen, it is Westerners like you who go out there but are not serious.'

'Rubbish!' argues Bruce. 'It is the Russians, most of whom are crooks anyway, who delay and delay.'

Mimi pauses, before striking. 'So Mr Clever English Businessman, if that what you think, why you want do business there anyway?'

'I don't particularly, but it's the Wild West out there and that's where you can make a killing if you strike the right deal – which is what I'm trying to do.'

Bruce smirks at me. I feign impartiality.

Mimi attacks again. 'You go there because you think you can *exploit us* but we are *not* stupid and if you double-cross us . . .' She makes a horizontal motion across her throat with her long and immaculate fingernails.

Bruce rolls his eyes in my direction.

Mimi continues, 'You do that in meeting in territories of former Soviet Union and you will *not* get contract but will be lucky to walk out. They expect *everybody* to show respect.'

The meeting is not going well: time for me to intervene.

'That does seem to me sound advice though I think, in fact I know, you would find Bruce comes across somewhat differently in an actual meeting.'

Unfortunately we are now into the second bottle, with Bruce ahead of Mimi and me. He does not take the hint. Instead he starts attacking me.

'This one is a lazy cunt! He earns a bloody great salary for doing the square root of bugger all most of the time. He swans around, buys some drinks for people and hey presto, he gets what he wants!'

'Actually, Bruce, if that were the case – and in fact it isn't – but I would have thought that was rather clever of me.'

But to my pleasure, it is Mimi who comes to my defence.

'I think you should show him more respect, for he knows more than you and you will need him for deals if you negotiate this way and you drink too much. Westerners all think Russians get drunk but they do deal sober and do not respect those who do not, at least in business. Take my word for it: you will get *done over* if you behave like this.'

When I leave with Bruce I say to her, 'I will see you tomorrow,' to which she replies with a 'maybe'. But the hug and kiss we exchange tells me that we will.

As we take the Tube together, Bruce says, 'Sorry about that mate, but she's wrong and bloody arrogant, thinks she knows it all when she's a bloody hooker.'

'That's as maybe but she also happens to be the most interesting and intelligent woman I have ever met and I love her.'

'Catherine the Great? You love fucking Catherine the Great!'

'Who was reputedly a great lover and a bloody interesting woman, so would have been wonderful to screw – provided she didn't chop your head off afterwards.'

With that we both laugh and the tension is gone.

I leave him and reflect on the fact that I am now, if possible, even more smitten with this woman. Not only can she much more than hold her own against my friend, but we are when together partners against an often hostile world. In the months ahead, we will meet other carefully selected members of my circle. I will much enjoy the feeling of being Mimi's partner and having her as mine. I am discreetly showing her off and relishing the experience.

As arranged, I see Mimi the next day.

'Your friend is *wanker* who thinks he knows it all; take my word, you will be lucky to get out not in concrete boots if he behave like that.'

The conversation moves to drugs.

'According to Bruce, the City of London is fuelled on coke and if they had genuine zero tolerance, the country's banking and finance system would collapse overnight.'

'Have you taken it?'

'No, not my thing – my addiction, my *only* addiction, is you, my love.'

'Do not say these things but I think you are clean-living, you do not gamble, you do not do drugs, you do not drink too much, unlike your friend of whom you must be careful, especially if you do business in former states of Soviet Union. He should not talk to you the way he does and he must not talk that way to my countrymen. Sometimes I think that despite you being so clever, I am your age and you are mine.'

'Mimi, I am a really nice bloke with a nasty mind.'

What I am thinking as I say this is that she is trying to warn me and protect me. She is showing love for me and it brings a light mist of tears to my eyes. I wonder whether she sees this as we look at one another, or that she notices that I sometimes gently weep as she makes me come.

After we have sex I say, 'There is one thing that concerns me. I never give you any pleasure. It is all one way.'

'Do you think I do not get enough sex? Forty per cent of women, even more my age, do not come. These things matter more to men, is not important.'

I am going on to chair a committee meeting. As I dress I comment, 'Here I go, reacquiring bourgeois respectability, garment by garment. If only they knew.'

She laughs and tells the maid, who grins when she sees me.

As I leave I tell Mimi that I love her.

'Maybe,' she says.

But I am absolutely certain that she knows I do, and I think she returns the sentiment. I am still, of course, a wanker, all men always will be, but I am less of a wanker than most and I am 'her' wanker or at least one of them. And I want her to love me.

This leads me to think about her pleasure and I decide the only thing I can sensibly do is not worry about it. I have raised it and I have my answer. To do so again would be boring and unproductive but it does concern me. What I conclude, rightly or wrongly, is that, in a business where she has to have intercourse so much of the time, the thing I can really do for her is not insist on penetration. As I desperately hope that our relationship will be a long one, that may come in the future when we go away together, to be kept as something special which lies ahead of us.

As I go home, it snows.

The trip to Minsk, Belarus happens only after Bruce has wrestled with bureaucracy and visited the embassy many times to obtain visas.

At the border, I reflect that time-wasting, pointless officialdom is everywhere. The border guard has a huge ring-binder. Their embassy in London has sent details of the fact that Bruce and I are due to enter Belarus here and now and he is checking us off on the list, his difficulty increased by the fact that our passports are not in Cyrillic but in Western script. Such individual checks generate long queues.

Minsk is all wide boulevards, grandiloquent architecture and open spaces: good, I think, for preventing conspiracies and stopping barricades.

Our hotel is in a large, dingy and down-at-heel 1960s building. At the reception staffed by disapproving, middle-aged *hausfraus*, I leave Bruce to sort out the fact that we appear to have booked four rather than two double rooms but do not have the compulsory medical insurance, and glance around. Sitting in the cavernous lobby are a middle-aged woman and a younger companion, who is sitting hunched forward in a peculiar way but who has stunningly beautiful eyes. We exchange smiles, hers ending this with a coy look downwards, before I move up some steps to an area with a dry, non-functioning fountain as its centrepiece.

A young woman approaches me. 'You stay this hotel?'

'Yes.'

'You Western businessman?'

'Yes.'

'You want I come to your room?'

'We're about to go out to dinner.'

'Later then, I come to your room, which number?'

'I'm not sure, my colleague's booking in.'

'I find you in bar, later.'

'Perhaps.'

I wander back to Bruce.

'I think I've just been propositioned,' I tell him.

'It's one of the hotel hookers, you're in the bloody Soviet

Union now, mate. Also, you're not allowed to bring anyone back to your room, so if you want that – 'cause you're a dirty bastard and you're away from Her Highness Catherine – you will have to choose a house tart, *le gâteau du château*, as you might say.'

At the excellent dinner, we are joined by Sergei, whom Bruce has set up as our man on the spot, and also by Tasha, whose large-nosed looks remind me of a pretty female version of Bruce.

'So this must be the Minsk girlfriend?'

'Not slept with her yet, and judging by the hotel rules won't get to this time, not unless I can sneak her in. We must get an apartment next time.'

Having all got to know one another and me having discussed Western business methods with Sergei whilst Bruce and Tasha exchange meaningful glances, we make our way back to the hotel and decide to have a drink in the bar. As Bruce finds the toilet, I go upstairs. Halfway up the wide piece of classic 1960s staircase, I am approached by a middle-aged woman who I recognise as the one sitting next to the pair of coy, beautiful eyes.

'You want woman?'

'Possibly.'

'You want me?'

I always feel that honesty is the best policy in these circumstances.

'No.'

'You like girl sitting next to me in lobby?'

'Oh, yes.'

She makes a barely visible hand movement and at the bottom of the stairs, the eyes appear. But from the top of the stairs, so does the other woman who spoke to me when we arrived.

The eyes are stationary, the accompanying body half

hidden by the stair rail, but the woman from the top is moving fast.

The middle-aged woman turns and issues an order.

'No, Olga.'

The advance on me from above turns to retreat.

'That is Irena, she will be at your room in half an hour.'

Which tells me how long Bruce and I have for a nightcap.

Actually it is probably nearer forty minutes but even so, I have literally just got into my room when there is a knock at the door.

Irena is a bit plump but has the height to carry it, being taller than me by about four inches. Anyway, it's really too late to back out now so we agree on $100, which Bruce has thoughtfully supplied in advance.

Irena says, 'You use bathroom, you take shower,' and I realise exactly who is in control.

When I am finished, she is behind the door as she says, 'Now I do same.'

Whilst I lie waiting for her, I think how coy she seems to be about showing me her body, especially given her profession, an impression reinforced by the fact that she turns off the light as she comes out of the bathroom before climbing into bed with me.

We begin to caress one another. I feel I am past the point of no return. Well past. What have I become? I am flouting the bourgeois conventions for which I now have contempt. I am having sex with a beautiful prostitute in one of the last remaining bastions of communism. What would those Conservative selectors think if they could see me now?

I relish the thought and it adds to my pleasure as she gives me a blow job straight out of a prostitute's training manual (though none rival Mimi, who simply knows me like the back of her hand).

I offer Irena the choice of position, but she sticks with the missionary.

Afterwards, before leaving she says, 'You like see me again tomorrow?'

'OK.'

I don't know what normal is any more.

'You are such a filthy, dirty bastard!'

'Bruce, it was offered to me on a plate.'

'You're still a filthy bastard. Fucking, filthy bastard.'

He returns to his sausage of unknown animal origin, conscience duly mollified.

After visiting a factory, which reminds me of the many dairy plants I have visited both as a businessman and politician, a late lunch with Sergei sees us turn to discussing the women of Belarus.

Bruce delivers his verdict: 'You know, mate, you can see why I'm never going out with an English bird ever again. The women of all these countries, there's just no comparison, English birds are short, fat and stroppy. Put any of these in London and they'd be considered beautiful, whereas here they're just average.'

I have to say that I could see his point: the young ones are quite simply some of the most beautiful women in the world; a shame they do not appear to age well.

Irena I see after this lunch. She waits for me and knocks just moments after I am back in my room. She is just as entertaining the second time and bizarrely takes one of our condoms and, from my eighth-storey room, bombs someone below with it, before rushing back to my bed, laughing. She is scarcely more than a child.

As we lie there attempting to talk, she takes my hand and lays it flat against her own, palm to palm.

'Is very little, you woman-man.'

I laugh, and she giggles.

When she has to go she asks me for some roubles in addition to the $100. This, I learn, is to pay off the ironing lady/concierge to the floor and the doorman downstairs. Apparently, these people impose what is effectively a movement tax on the working girls.

TWENTY-TWO

'Giving her control is my gift to her'

B ack at Gatwick, whilst I am deciding which perfume I
think Mimi would prefer, Bruce comments, 'That one
looks pretty cheesy to me, mate.'

'I think I want cheesy, because she has a hard life and I
do not think she has had enough cheese in it.'

Because we are more or less the only customers, the
cashier is listening. She laughs and when I pay she smiles at
me and says of the tall, elegant DKNY I have selected,
'Good choice, I hope she likes it.'

Of course, because it is the one that most appeals to me
I buy two and give both my women the same.

When I get home, H asks, 'Good trip?'

'Yes, certainly had its moments.'

'Sleep with anyone?'

Fishing out her perfume, I reply, 'I've got something for you.'

'I'll take that as a "yes", then.'

But she still seems to appreciate the present, as does
Mimi, who asks no questions about my sex life but tells me
that her boyfriend has taken away her dog.

'What do you mean taken him away? Surely he can't just do that?'

'He say, and he is right, that dog doesn't go with life of working girl. I have one customer, I leave him to go to bathroom. When I come back bed has been occupied by dog, who is growling at him. Another customer, he arrive but when he see pit bull in flat, he says he has changed his mind and goes. Also I have to walk him every day and he needs lots of exercise so my boyfriend find new home for him.'

As she tells me this, I think, what an utter shit, he gives her a dog, allows her long enough to grow really fond of the child substitute and then, just when she has fallen in love with it, takes it away.

'That doesn't strike me as a very nice or affectionate way to treat you.'

The next time I go round, I take her a dog – made out of chocolate, for it is near Easter and I manage to find a lugubrious-faced, edible canine.

As ever, she does not thank me but rushes off to the maid saying, 'Look what he has given me,' and I know she really appreciates it.

At the House of Commons, I go to the souvenirs kiosk and buy her their little bear with the House of Commons logo on him. Next time I see her, I give this to her.

'Just had to buy it for you because, you see, I had this vision: you can put the little bear in the paws of your Siberian tiger.'

'Good boy, that is right way round. For my mother say, I am little tyrant.'

'I know, do you think I am unaware of these things? It is part of the reason I love you, though what that says about my own fucked-up psychology is a different issue.'

'Actually I am not tiger but dragon. In Chinese astrology I am fire dragon. You read it. That is exactly what I am like.'

I google Chinese astrology and learn all about the Dragon. Mimi knows herself well. Dragons are certainly fiery and know exactly what they want and how to get it. But they also have a warm heart and a natural charm. I learn that the most compatible match for a Dragon is the Monkey or the Rat. I am happy to discover that I am a Monkey.

'Can you go to prison for debt?'

I laugh.

'Once we had the harshest regime in the world, the English debtors' prison where you were trapped because you couldn't work to pay off your debt, so without kindly friends or relations, you could languish in there for decades in a terrible catch-22. But we don't live in the eighteenth century any more, so now I am pleased to say the answer is no.'

'So you would not go there for parking tickets?'

'I don't think so. Why?'

'I just wonder what happen if you have many parking tickets and you do not pay them and they mount up. Can you go to prison?'

'In principle, no, they are a civil not a criminal offence.'

'So why anybody pay? Why do people not just ignore tickets?'

'Firstly because it affects your credit record and that for respectable people is a pain, but also eventually, especially if there are enough of them, you are pursued. They send the bailiffs after you.'

'But what if you do not let them in?'

'It's not just a case of a polite knock at the door and they go away again. Or at least it may be like that the first time, but not later. As I understand it, the debt is sold and the debt collection agency only get their money if they manage to extract it, which means they carry on. Eventually, if necessary, they distrain your goods.'

By this stage we are undressed on the bed. I lie stretched before her. My arms are either behind my head or stretched out, whilst the position of my feet adds to the Christ-like pose. She sits above me, still in bra and knickers, dominant. I stroke her as we talk. Then I lean forward and kiss her feet, noting, as I always do, the long, prehensile toes. My actions are submissive and placatory for I know she is in control, though I have chosen to give it to her for that is what I want. It is also something I can do for her. Giving her control is my gift to her. Using it wisely to stimulate me but not taking it too far is her gift to me; part of the exquisite mutual rewarding of gentle dominatrix and mild submissive. They are games that H has no interest in.

Why do I want to play them? Why do I never seek full sex with her? As I said to her of her boyfriend so early in our relationship, look back to infantile patterns of experience to understand middle-aged patterns of desire and satisfaction – a conclusion which must involve parents and siblings.

'What this word 'distrain' mean?' she demands. 'How many times I've told you, this is not House of Commons.'

'Sorry, but it's the technical term. In simple terms, they come into your flat and seize whatever they want to, computer, TV, hi-fi, even a car, taking however much they think is needed to cover the debt.'

'What am I going to do with you?'

She takes out a condom and rolls it on. My hand threads its way between her legs. As her tongue starts to lick up and down, I use the ball of my thumb to massage her crotch. She is on top and in control. Like some overpowering, beautiful, black widow, her arms and hands pin me down. Her legs control my arm and I fantasise that she could probably fairly easily break my wrist with her thighs if she chose to. As I grow more excited she uses her long, sharp, elegant nails to prick my scrotum. The action is on the cusp between pleasure and pain, but her tongue ensures this merely adds to the intensity.

I briefly look up to watch my own pleasure.

'Do not watch me in this way. I do not like it. Look down.'

Her nails stab me extra hard to ensure obedience.

I obey and then begin to groan and thresh as I come. She knows that this is no signal to stop. I remain entangled and restricted in her long, slim, elegant yet strong arms and legs, as my black widow carries on milking me past the point where I am producing anything, carrying me into a realm of exquisite sensitivity. I roll over but still she does not stop, instead using her other hand to dig her nails into my flesh.

'Oh God, oh Christ!' I cry.

'Ah, you think of him, now! But I have told you before to be quiet. Why you do not understand? Why will you not do as you are told!'

She smacks me, then, inspired, takes a paddle from the wall and brings it down on my bottom three or four times before adding several more smacks.

'I adore and worship you, beautiful woman that I love.'

And that is my exact sentiment. For my black widow is simultaneously the spider and the caped but beautiful widow of a pension-fund advert!

In Walt Disney's *Snow White*, I always thought the eponymous heroine a wimp, whereas her stepmother, the wicked queen, was vastly the more attractive and sexy figure. Oh, to be her victim!

It is an issue at the heart of Western culture for, in *Paradise Lost*, as Milton realised to his own horror, the

Christian God the story is supposed to glorify is a prat, while the devil is the appealing figure. Good cannot be separated from evil and, as on Orwell's farm where pigs and men become indistinguishable, one side cannot be separated from the other.

Why I am retreating from politics? Because I can no longer tell the two sides apart. My enemies are from my own party: we vie for the same things. I admire and enjoy the company of my opponents. After twenty years, it has become time for me to concentrate on the pleasures of intimacy and sexuality denied by my education and diverted into a futile pursuit of a public position I thought it my duty to seek. In short, I am bloody well enjoying myself and, if my fantasies seem somewhat juvenile and I am giving to Mimi the role of omnipotent mother, at once nurturing and gently disciplining, then I will. I am healing myself in the only way I think I know how.

Later that same evening, at around eleven o'clock, H and I are discussing whether it is time for bed when my mobile goes. It is a text: 'Hi its Mimi i have problem but cant ask nobody else. I need 5000£ and its an emergency. I will pay them back in 1.5 month. Can you help me.'

We talk on the phone. The conversation is entirely practical. I never ask her why she needs so much money so quickly, but tell her that although the money itself is no problem, such sums are paid by people like me in the form of a cheque.

She tells me it needs to be cash because the money is not for her and will take too long to clear through her bank account.

I ask her how much will be enough in the first instance. The answer is £2,000, which I promise to deliver when we meet at the barriers of a central London Tube station at two o'clock the following day.

In the morning, I test the limits of my access to cash. It begins well. A Tube station cashpoint coughs up £500 from one of my accounts. The same card provides another £500 at the other end of my journey. I know a third attempt will fail and it does. The machine refers me back to my card-issuer. On to card number two. I know the limit on this is less and £300 is the maximum yield.

I ring Freddy and casually inquire where he is, which turns out to be abroad for a conference, lucky chap.

I mentally run through a list of friends and contacts. Clearly anyone I approach is going to ask why I want the money. Eliminating those I cannot tell and those I would not wish to tell even though I could, I arrive at the godfather of one of my sons.

'Can you give me a thousand pounds in cash later this morning? I'll write you a cheque to cover it but I need cash.'

'Not sure, why do you need it?'

'Not on the phone, I'll tell you when I see you.'

Eventually he agrees to loan me the money. When I meet him he hands me an envelope containing £500 – all he could get out of the bank – and I give him a cheque before he asks what it's for. I explain.

'Giving her money is fine, but I should steer clear of the boyfriend, who anyway sounds like a pimp to me, if I were you.'

'She says not.'

'She would, wouldn't she!'

Mimi has always kept me waiting but this time it is only about five minutes.

As she walks towards me I notice the eyes of other men tracking her to see who will have the pleasure of the company of such a beautiful woman. She leans down to allow me to kiss her chastely on the cheeks, for I know she frowns upon public displays of affection.

What she is wearing includes a brooch, scarf and T-shirt I have given her which is, I suspect, entirely deliberate but I know it will not be mentioned.

We go to a nearby coffee shop.

She tells me her boyfriend is in a police cell.

'But that can't be just about some parking tickets. I checked with a lawyer friend of mine after we spoke to see that I'd given you the right advice. You don't go to prison or get arrested for unpaid parking tickets or congestion charges. What did he do?'

'In my country, we know nothing of bailiffs and all that. They do not exist. So, after I leave you, I ring him to tell him what you say and that it will be OK. He's happy and he go back to his flat but when he gets there, these bailiffs they are waiting for him.'

She tells me they end up calling the police because her boyfriend got angry.

'He ends up in cell and police check up on him and he have all these unpaid tickets and charges.'

'Not five thousand pounds' worth.'

'No. More!'

'How much?'

'Eight thousand pounds.'

'You're joking.'

'Do I look as if I am being funny?'

'How the fuck do you run up debts like that from parking tickets, for goodness sake?'

'You know these things. You don't pay forty, fifty pound, they double it then it become two-fifty. You get frightened so you just ignore it and they all go on going up. Is easy.'

'How's he taking it?'

'I worry for him. He hates be confined. He not good in enclosed spaces.'

I ask, 'Does he know where you're getting the money from?'

'He specifically tell me not to ask you but I have no one else. His friends are no good. They will not help. I ask other girls. They say if it few hundred pounds they can help but not amount like this. They send money home to families. They not have money in this country.'

'I know. One of the things I've always admired about you, one of the reasons I love you and know you are a good person, is that I know you send money back to your parents and your sister.'

'They always asking for money. They all phone me and say, "Don't tell others, but can you spare me another few hundred pounds here?" and then few hundred pounds there. They say, "We cannot pay this bill," or "We need money for that bill," – but I need some money for myself. I have to have life too.'

We discuss how she will raise the rest of the money to cover the debt. In the end, we agree that I will give her all she needs. The trust between us is such that I know she will not ask for more than that.

I discover that my account will allow me to withdraw up to £1,000 cash per day. So the following week she gets £3,000. She also gets a present.

'You know I have given you the Siberian tiger which is you and the little bear to go in her paws which is me? Well, now I have found you him, your boyfriend!'

What I hand her is a picture. It is one of those surreal 1920s advertisements for an obscure brand of Italian liquor which is pictured being enjoyed by a large hairy ape, who is knocking it back with abandon using his right hand whilst his left hangs down in front of his crotch.

'Don't tell me he isn't wanking himself with his left hand.

Mentioning which, did he ask you again where it's coming from – the money, I mean?'

'What do you think?'

'He could play it one of two ways.'

'I say to him, "Where do you think?"'

'Am I going to get any of it back, by the way? Money for you is one thing but giving money to your boyfriend is another.'

'You are not giving it to him, you are giving it to me, and I will make him sell his car.'

'But doesn't he drive you around in it, taking you to and from appointments? You really wouldn't look very good on the back of a tandem!'

She laughs.

'I can take taxis.'

The other £3,000 she gets the week after.

And finally, after I have come and am lying being cleaned with a baby wipe, I ask the questions which have been nagging in my mind for ages.

'Is he your pimp and did he traffic you here?'

'I find these questions insulting.'

'But nonetheless I want some answers.'

'No, he is my boyfriend. I order him around. He drives for me and does what I tell him. He does not get sex very often. You get it with me much more than he does. His friends, many of them do not like me. They tell him I am Hitler who boss him around. They call me his boss. He find this difficult. And, no, I was not trafficked. Can you imagine anyone trying to traffic me? I came here because I want to, for though is *shitty* country with many stupid rules, is better than mine. Is run by people like you but you also do what I say.'

I get up from the bed. She goes over to the wall, takes down a long cattle whip and flicks it at my buttocks.

'Ouch, that actually hurt.'

'One day, I am going to properly thrash you and you will not know before that it is going to happen. You are my laboratory rat.'

Still naked, I turn and kneel in front of her. I kiss her feet then move up to kiss her inner thighs. My arms entwine around her legs and I kiss her crotch through the translucent gauze of the immaculate La Perla knickers. She pushes me away.

'Do not do these things.'

At that moment I am both a worthless worm and a god with his goddess who is also a whore. And we both know I will do only what she, the boss, will allow.

TWENTY-THREE

'You've never really felt loved'

Another trip to the Baltics, this time at Keith's instigation, for he is to marry a nineteen-year-old Lithuanian girl he met in a Vilnius club. She is pregnant and they seem very much in love.

We are returning for the wedding. Keith is, as ever, a considerate host and he meets us at the airport. He has also found us an apartment we are to share with another of his friends who is arriving later. Cases dropped (men don't bother to unpack in such circumstances), we venture into the night.

Keith's stag night in a cavernous bar and then a university student hang-out is disappointing and I tell Bruce I want to go somewhere else, though I am happy to do this by myself, and know where I plan to go – a nightclub with integral pole dancing. He is in need of cash, which I have agreed to supply, so he comes with me if only to the hole in the wall.

I have just taken out the money and am giving him half when a Lithuanian girl approaches us out of the night.

'It is sister's birthday. She party in nightclub and I need go in but I have no money and cannot. Can you have ten litas?'

As this is all of two pounds, I simply give it to her with a smile and say, 'Have a nice night.'

Bruce and I part and I walk to my chosen venue. I am paying ten litas on the door when I feel a tap on the shoulder. I wonder whether Bruce has decided to join me but turn to see the girl of moments before.

'You not go here but you like come with me?'

I turn, she takes my hand and we go back into the night.

'You have apartment near here?'

'Yes.'

'You take there, we have sex.'

I have still not properly seen her for the club entrance was dim, but the jeans and T-shirt-clad figure looks great and the face is attractive enough in the lamplight. She reminds me of girls who would not sleep with me at Oxford, which makes me pleased.

'We taxi and need condom, you pay.'

'Great, no problem.'

As she leads me by the hand she says, 'I amateur, not professional. I student, two hundred litas.'

'That will be just fine.'

She is completely in charge as we find a taxi and are taken to a late-night shop, where I buy her cigarettes and a soft drink as well as the condoms, and we are soon back in my apartment. She looks around it and smiles her approval whilst I look at her and smile mine: she is about my height and must be a size eight with a lovely figure and a pretty face, albeit with a few spots around the chin.

We begin to kiss, our tongues penetrating one another's mouths, then move on to fondling and rubbing. Condom-encased, I enter her first with her on top and then with me.

Afterwards, she asks if she can smoke, which I allow, though I would actually prefer she didn't – at least not in the bedroom. However to refuse would seem churlish. I have still not paid her so I avoid her needing to ask by taking 400 litas from my wallet.

'You'll need a taxi,' I say.

This earns a final kiss on the lips and her name and telephone number before, clad in my Chinese silk dressing gown, I escort her out.

The following morning, we have to drive the length of the country to reach the wedding venue by 3 p.m. Keith's side are to travel in convoy and, perhaps inevitably because of the night before, it starts off late.

As we near our destination, Bruce's mobile grows ever more animated, most of the calls coming from Egla, his London-based Lithuanian girlfriend who is back in her native country acting as cultural go-between for the English and Lithuanian contingents.

We are late and Egla is not happy. She may be almost ten years younger than Bruce and banking on him to provide the Western husband and lifestyle to which she aspires, but she berates him and sulks like a secure wife when we arrive at the provincial registry office. This seems to me scarcely fair as it is primarily Keith's show, but in such circumstances logic is of little relevance as she wants to let off steam at someone.

Egla looks us up and down, scowls, clicks her tongue, brushes some imaginary fluff from Bruce's lapels and hurries us in to where the bride is already waiting.

We are unfamiliar with the etiquette so Egla has to explain what is going on.

The bride's party and the groom's party line up on either side of a long white room. This has amusing implications for, immediate family aside, all Keith's guests are English males between 25 and 50, and almost all hers are teenage girls and women in their early twenties. The result as the two sides look one another up and down is somewhat comic.

Bruce whispers, 'It's like a Russian bride selection event, we must do one of those sometime.'

Elga is talking in English but I am not paying any real attention as my eyes are on a slim, pale-faced brunette wearing a bright red figure-hugging dress. Bruce, despite the proximity of Egla, is doing something similar and we agree that she and her green-attired companion are the best of what is on show.

After the ceremony, complete with comically pregnant bride, we pose for endless photographs and then move on to the reception in yet another Wild West bar, which is all pine and adorned by nineteenth-century farm implements.

The feasting which follows is on a truly impressive scale: we start with a selection of canapés and light foods but there is so much of this course that it could feed the entire party on its own. It includes local delicacies such as pig's ear, at which most of the English, though not Bruce or me, turn up their noses. One of the English guests, who in her person confirms all Bruce's opinions about English girls in comparison with their Eastern European counterparts, makes silly noises of disgust. I consider making a remark but decide against, though I would not be impressed if I were one of our Lithuanian hosts – how bloody rude the English can be.

There is then a brief recess before the revels properly begin. Drink lubricates and loosens inhibitions, and soon the parties begin to mingle. The bride's brother becomes drunk, morose and then threatening. The English men have their collective stereotype of a people of stunning women and idiot men reinforced. Speeches are made: the best man has the good sense to tell stories of Keith's misspent youth but to avoid any controversial topics.

A disco and male singer appear. Photographs are being taken and that gives me an opportunity for a picture with the girl in the red dress. The Lithuanian girls have the usual collective problem that the one who takes the photograph is always omitted from the picture. Ever the gentleman, I solve it for them and then have my own picture taken with them by Bruce, who has cottoned on to the idea.

The ice now well and truly broken, red-dress and I begin to dance and talk. She is a theatre and media student and we discuss her ambitions as well as my political experiences. Reluctantly I decide that propositioning her will, in all the circumstances, be too much even for me.

One reason is that I also talk to Egla. Courtesy of Bruce, she knows all about me and doesn't approve – of me or Mimi. My defence that my wife knows and accepts is not really believed and I gather there is nothing I can say to change that. She also does not approve of prostitution and is condemnatory of the women that do it.

Aware that she is putting them in a separate category to be reviled, I remind her, 'Prostitutes are women too, you know! With all the same feelings, emotions and needs that you have. They are aware of what society thinks of them and that actually means that doing what they do takes courage, a lot more than you might think.'

'Do you love Mimi?'

'As it happens, yes I do.'

'How *can* you love woman like that?'

'Because I don't think what she does is wrong and because it is your wretched Catholicism which traditionally gives women only two roles: Madonna or whore, and of the two, I prefer the latter.'

We are, however, still talking – she doesn't feel me to be so sacrilegious and subversive to the point where she can no longer speak to me – when the idea comes to use the hotel sauna and pool. This gives us the chance to see red-dress, green-dress and the English cousins all in a bikini or bra and pants depending upon whether they have had the foresight to pack a costume. Inevitably the Lithuanians have a swimming costume and the English girls do not, though I, like most of the other English men, have brought trunks.

My resolve not to make a pass at red-dress wavers but, reflecting what a public fool I could make of myself, common sense reasserts itself. I have come to feel that I am the flag-bearer for English good manners. Egla, who is equally trim, slim and attractive, declines to follow the English example and does not join us because she has no costume.

At the reception I meet a friend of Keith's, a gentleman of about my own age called Madhev to whom I take a shine. He has an interest in psychology and is an admirer of Jung. He will be coming back to Riga with us.

I persuade Bruce to perform his Elvis impersonation. This is a great success and ushers in a series of performances including from the Lithuanian girls. Of course, the English cousins do not perform.

The dance floor enables me to take the girl in the red dress in my arms and to kiss her. When I leave I have her telephone number, though wonder if and when I will have the opportunity to use it. Its value is enhanced by the fact that the younger, taller, fitter Brummie who is pursuing her friend fails to acquire hers. I do wonder whether my own behaviour is becoming increasingly juvenile.

Should I really be trying to pick up students young enough to be my daughter? I don't really care. Not at all.

The following day there is a huge collective breakfast at which much alcohol is again on offer, though I cannot have any because I will be driving. I see red-dress now in skintight jeans and kiss her goodbye more than once.

We leave the coast for Riga but before we can do so, Bruce must be introduced to Egla's sister, who was not at the wedding but has come to collect her. Unfortunately she is slightly delayed, during which time Bruce falls asleep on the sofa in our sitting room.

As a consequence, when the sister arrives to be introduced, I play the gentleman, leap to my feet, extend my hand, smile and introduce myself whilst Bruce snores. I call to him but he never really surfaces before Egla and her sister turn on their heels and walk out.

A short time later, he gets a text: 'You disrespect my sister, she think your friend my boyfriend.'

His attempts to call back and make peace go unanswered.

'I was fucking asleep,' he explains to us before resuming his slumbers in the car, which allows me to begin to talk to Madhev while I drive.

'I gather you're something of a Jungian guru.'

'It's an image I like, though I'm not a trained psychiatrist.'

'Jung's good on the midlife crisis isn't he?'

'Yes.'

'Well, I've got a whole load of that.'

And then I begin to talk, almost without ceasing: about my own behaviour of the last few years, my feelings about the Conservative party, my consorting with prostitutes.

Slowly the conversation focuses on H.

'When we married, she was much more experienced than me. She'd slept with lots of blokes but the great love of her life had been a relationship with somebody else's husband ever since she was a student.

'H and I worked together. She wasn't much impressed by me, a short, plumpish and rather verbose ex-public schoolboy. Despite her lack of interest, the needs of a mutual client ensured she had to see a fair amount of me. I knew she wasn't impressed so I didn't ask her out but was just friendly.

'That summer, the trade unions were engaged in one of their periodic bouts of striking to try to destabilise Margaret Thatcher's hated government. The transport unions regularly brought both the underground and mainline rail services to a halt. The firm organised car-sharing and, as H lived nearby, I took the opportunity to offer her a lift. This worked even better than I hoped. By pure coincidence it turned out that she was planning to stay with a uni friend at exactly the time I was on holiday in the same area.

'Realising the railways would be on strike and finding all the coaches full, H accepted my offer of a lift. Over eight or nine hours both ways I tried to talk my way into her knickers, not that I succeeded at first. When I delivered her back to her London flat, she effectively told me to get lost.

'But she was impressed when a couple of days later, I asked her for the right petrol money. Silly, really, but she thought that if I didn't ask her for it or asked too little, then I was a creep, and if I asked too much I was exploiting her, but if I asked what she'd been told was the right figure, she could respect me.

'I then left it another week before making one last attempt. This time she said yes. We went to bed more or less straight away and began living together two days later. So I'm pretty put out when, three weeks later coming up to a Bank Holiday weekend, she says, "I've got an old boyfriend coming so I want you out whilst he's here."

'I turned up on the Monday evening as instructed, undecided whether to end it there. It all depended upon what she said. I'm sure she realised this 'cause she came to the door in just a kimono, said just the right thing about how when she'd slept with him she'd thought of me, and we instantly made love in the same sheets she'd used with him just hours if not minutes before.

'Thereafter he came to our wedding and then, when she is a full-time mother and I'm out working all day to support her and the family, she has him come and spend the day with her, arriving after I've left and leaving before I return. It happens three or four times a year. I never ask what they do but certainly the opportunity is there.'

'And you allowed this to happen?' asked Madhev. 'Most husbands would have put their foot down.'

'Well I didn't, I just put up with it. Anyway, some years later, we go to stay with him and his children one weekend when his wife's away. On the Saturday, she looks after the children, while he and I go out and get pissed and I discover he's a really nice guy. The following day, roles are reversed and she goes off with him. She turns up hours later with a broad grin on her face.

'As I am driving home, once the boys are asleep I think, shall I ask her? I know they could have as he has a separate little flat nearby and that look on her face . . . well. But all I eventually do is say, "I don't ask questions to which I don't want to know the answer."'

Madhev considers this. 'You realise this is the means by which she controls you. She uses sex and him to remind you every so often who is the boss.'

Then he asks about my childhood.

'Oh, my mother suffered post-natal depression after my birth and she's a very unmaternal woman in any case. I never remember her cuddling me but I do remember being afraid of her and her slapping me. My father tried to compensate, as did my elder sister.'

Madhev delivers his judgement. 'You've never really felt loved. You still don't. H exacerbated that by being controlling.

You were always the supplicant for sex and, of course, the irony is that it is always the partner who doesn't want it or isn't bothered who controls the sexual side of any relationship.'

But I also realise something else. I have been and am busy rewriting my youth. I am giving myself the adolescent adventures, the young man's affairs, the flirtation with danger I never had at the time. Bruce says it is the reason I am so 'fucking' liberal in my attitudes towards my sons and so gross in my own behaviour. I believe it should be allowed, precisely because I never had it and what I am doing now is trying to make up for it. He may be right but I do not really care about my motivation, for every experience I have ever had tells me that the world is a better place if people are allowed to enjoy themselves as much as possible without significantly damaging others.

And most politicians spend most of the time trying to do the opposite: imposing unnecessary restrictions which demonstrate too little trust in people and too little understanding that if you offer perverse incentives, people will rapidly and continuously behave perversely.

One border crossing and four hours later, we arrive in Riga in the darkness. I am tired, emotionally as well as physically, because driving is difficult in this foreign city with Bruce giving directions from a small-scale and ill-lit map.

Suddenly there is a large police armoured car coming towards me at speed with lights flashing, on my side of the road. I swerve towards the kerb to avoid it only to hear the rasp of metal on metal.

'What the fuck are you doing?' shouts Bruce and I now see the bus.

'Just drive, for fuck's sake, drive!' shouts Bruce and I follow his order.

There is another sound of scraping metal as the bus and I part. I cannot leave the scene quickly enough, but once we are a couple of streets away, I can scarcely any longer drive I am shaking so much.

'Do you think we should –'

'I don't think a Latvian police cell is a very nice place to be, do you?'

I try to speak again, but Bruce shouts me down. 'Just carry on driving, will you, while I find the fucking flat.'

Mercifully, we reach it just a few minutes later.

We look at the side of the car. The damage seems not to be as bad as I feared, though in the darkness it is not easy to tell.

Bruce phones Keith to sort out the keys but has to add, '. . . and you'll never guess what happened to us. He only crashed into a fucking bus.'

'That's really not kind,' I say.

But he has to give Keith a brief account of the incident. After he hangs up I tell him, 'Look, I've had accidents before, so I know I'm suffering from shock and I'm good for nothing now for at least the next hour.'

He and Madhev conclude I need food and drink. We go out to a restaurant and after dinner Madhev, who is staying separately from us at a hotel, leaves us.

But for Bruce the night is young and, with him as the decision-taker, we are soon back in his favourite karaoke bar, where he again appears as Elvis, and lo and behold the same Latvian female fan is there.

He is happy.

'Why don't you ring Sofia?' he suggests, and I do, but she doesn't answer or respond to a text.

Much beer, singing and conversation later, I say, 'Afraid this is too much akin to hell in my current state. I want to go.'

He is reluctant to part from his Latvian but I insist. We go on to a club then a bar. I have switched to soft drinks but Bruce stays on the alcohol.

'I'm hungry,' he says.

'You can't be.'

'Need something to soak up all the alcohol, mate. In this country they have a chain of twenty-four-hour food places. Can't remember the name but I know there's one near our flat.'

We are soon there. He orders a large plate of food but is more interested in the brandy I have bought.

Even though it is now the small hours of the morning, we are not the only customers – and some seem interested in us. We are joined by four young men. The one girl with them stays apart, however, sitting at a separate table. Soon I am buying rounds of cognac, though I leave my own largely untouched, and we are discussing Latvia, Riga and the ethnic divide between 'Latvian Latvians' and 'Russian Latvians' like them. There is much heartiness but also an underlying air of menace.

Then one of them says, 'You want my sister?'

I assume this means the girl who is sitting separately from them.

'No, thank you.'

Though, if truth be told, I do, because she is tall, blonde and attractive. She is in fact exactly what I want, but . . .

Bruce suddenly says, 'The situation in this country at this point is extremely complicated. One has to be aware of incipient tensions and the violence which can often result from failure to anticipate the needs and aspirations of the different groups involved, particularly when it comes to the direct financial effects of certain classes of action.'

'What is he talking about?' I ask myself, and then I realise this is code for the fact that we are in a nasty situation: what if they decide, perhaps as we leave, that our wallets and passports are more valuable to them than to us?

'So what would you identify as the key means to take the agenda forward?' I ask, getting into the spirit of the thing.

'Precipitate action can often be unwise. Satisfying consumer requirements can often be the best short-term means to mitigate the demands of discontented peoples.'

'Do you think the essential political direction from this point is to the left or rightwards, I mean in the immediate term?'

'Undoubtedly leftward,' he replies, and I assume he understands that I can't remember which direction the flat is.

I buy more brandy. The number of glasses on the table is beginning to be truly impressive. Further supplies delivered, I go to the toilet, lock myself in, remove my shoes and deposit the entire contents of my wallet less one credit card and about 40 lats in their heels. The result is uncomfortable but at least feels more secure.

When I return, Bruce is continuing to entertain the men: '. . . of course, the impact of the mercenary is not to be underestimated. For instance, the role of Serbians as guns for hire is known to all those doing business in Eastern Europe . . .'

Is he trying to tell them we are rich enough to have bodyguards a short call away?

The response is interesting.

'You perhaps have jobs for us in such role?'

'We'll think about it,' I say.

'We'll need contact details,' says Bruce.

These we are given.

'Well, my good friends, the night is no longer young,' says Bruce. I offer them another round of brandy which they accept and I buy before, with many smiles, much hand-shaking and back-slapping and assurances of friendship, we leave. Casually sauntering towards the door, we turn briskly to the left once through it and then, a few yards down the road, break into a run to the flat, though whether you can describe Bruce's motion in all of this as anything more than a stagger is questionable.

He has the key but I have to let us in, at which point he falls towards me with the words, 'I am completely and utterly *fucked.*'

I steer Bruce to one of the foldaway beds, loosen his tie, take off his shoes, watch him instantly fall into a drunken stupor and hope he doesn't piss himself in his sleep for, I think, I will be the one who has to clear it up.

As for myself, I do not feel sleepy but go onto the Internet, turning to the Riga guidebook. One of the advantages of this Protestant city is that the sex industry is entirely open and above board. Unlike their innocent Lithuanian equivalents, Latvians are seldom if ever mentioned in trafficking stories. I wonder whether a more open and public industry does not actually impede the possibility of exploiting the innocent.

I phone 'Model escorts'.

'Hello, do you speak English?'

'Yes.'

'I picked you because I like girls with model figures and that's what I am looking for, tall and slim.'

'With a pretty face?'

'Yes.'

Half an hour later, I let her in. She is everything I had hoped for: a pretty, slim blonde, a student at Riga University, following in the footsteps of her older sister who made money the same way. She does most of the work but with a new variation. She is something of a hippie chick and she sings incantations over me. The working women of Riga, as ever, do not let me down.

I am intrigued when I see her take the used condom containing my sperm, tie a knot in the end and put it in her handbag.

'What on earth are you doing?'

She smiles heart-breakingly sweetly, for she is truly lovely, and says:

'What your name again?'

I tell her.

'Lots of little –'

'Pardon?'

'Full of your babies. I can sell this down road, I make extra ten lats.'

This is weird. Am I now in a Latvian sperm bank?

Having seen her out, I fall asleep, only to wake three hours later to hear the sound of fists pounding on the door, then a splintering and cracking of wood. As I begin to rise the bedroom door is thrown open by black-uniformed Uzi-carrying policemen. Once they are in the room, one of them begins to draw a baton.

'Driving away from accident and abusing purity of Latvian women are serious offences, very serious offences,' he begins.

'I didn't realise prostitution was a crime here. I thought it was legal and as for the accident, it was because of your armoured car.'

But the baton is already descending towards my groin.

I am covered in sweat as I struggle to . . .

It is one of those nightmares that seems so real at the moment of waking that it is sheer relief to discover it is only a dream.

Once I have composed myself, I check on Bruce to ensure he has not choked in his own vomit or drowned in his piss, then I look at my watch and see it is morning.

I go out. Having seen a lovely shoe and boot shop right

next to our block, I phone H. 'Hi, it's me, I'm just checking your shoe size.'

Then I phone Mimi. 'Hi, it's me, I just need to check your shoe size.'

Finally I phone my father. 'I'm in Riga, there's limited credit on my Latvian SIM and I want to talk to you so please can you ring me back?'

'That'll cost me a fortune, won't it?' he objects.

'Probably, but I want to talk to you and I'm worth it.'

I tell him about the car journey and the conclusions.

'Yes,' he says. 'I'd pretty much figured all that out for myself. The point is that she *did* love you, your mother, she always loved you. You know, her own childhood . . . well, as you know, it wasn't very good itself or very loving and she wasn't taught to display it, but she did her best. She did love you, she just wasn't very good at showing it.'

My eyes are watering. I say, 'It never felt like that.'

TWENTY-FOUR

'At some stage, the shit is going to hit the fan'

Back in London, I deliver the boots to my respective partners and tell them about my trip; the details are, of course, edited appropriately for each of them

As usual Mimi does not say thank you but she does reveal that she cares about me. After hearing my story, she laughs at me and calls me an idiot, saying, 'You begin to understand. My country is dangerous place. And I don't want you go there and do stupid things. And another thing . . .'

Then, she proceeds to have a go at me about how I just want her as a mistress. As always, she's found something to tell me off about. Her point seems valid to me because it raises the difficult question about our future together: am I going to leave my wife for her?

As she talks at me, I wonder what I am going to say. How do I get out of this one? I think. Then I know.

'We could run away together and I could probably just about afford it. But in all honesty, it's not what I think you want, at least not at this stage. And I also know that for your sake, I mustn't treat my wife badly.'

'Why you say that?'

'Because, if I treat her badly now, then I might treat you badly in the future. And you will not have me if I am not a decent bloke. I have to behave properly to both of you or I will end up with nothing!'

'Clever boy, you're learning. I have to know you will not run off with next pretty, slim brunette that comes along.'

And at this point she smacks me, but it is very half-hearted. I reflect that she must love me because she is scarcely any more able to hit me than I was able to abuse the 'schoolgirl' when I was playing at being DH Lawrence's nineteenth-century schoolmaster. When I phone my father to tell him about this conversation he confirms my belief.

'She must love you because she always seems to be bollocking you,' he says.

'And that's what women do, is it?'

'Yes, at least in my experience.'

'Well, you know they say a man cannot serve two masters. That may be true but I reckon he can serve two mistresses!'

As we finish our conversation, my father tells me he would like to meet Mimi at some point.

'I'll see what I can arrange,' I say. 'Something should be possible as I think our lives are going to become ever more mingled.'

But even as I am uttering the words I am wondering how this will be possible. How will a life together combine with the one I already have with H?

After presenting H with her boots, which are the tartier of the two pairs, I tell her about the wedding. Then I cannot stop myself going on to tell her about the car journey and Madhev's remarks. She says, 'Actually I didn't have sex with my ex. I haven't had anyone else since three weeks into our relationship, and I wasn't controlling. It just wasn't like that.'

She has tears in her eyes and we hug and kiss. Later she adds, 'I'm sorry if I hurt you, I didn't mean to, but you were so bumptious and it was the only way I could stop you being uppity, take you down a peg or two. And I do love you, you know, I always have, I'm just not always terribly good at showing it. And I just find sex . . . well, difficult. I only do it out of love for you and anyway, you can hardly complain because you've had a whale of a time – talk about having your cake and eating it. Though am I the cake or the eating?'

'The cake, I think. They are the eating.'

But I also think, without saying it, that her comment about stopping me being uppity means she *was* actually being controlling, or at least trying to be. Meanwhile, she is still talking, asking me a question.

'And among all of them, you must have a favourite; who's your favourite?'

So I tell her about Mimi.

'Do you love her?'

'Yes, I'm afraid I do, very, very much.'

'And do you still love me?'

'Yes, I do, though, after twenty years, in a rather different way.'

'Then I suppose you'd better have us both, then. I *am* prepared to share you but I have to be the senior wife, like in Islam, and it's going to cost you *a lot*, so you'd better get earning if you're going to deliver to us both.'

'I think I know the arrangement I want. Each of you in her own flat and I could swap between you.'

'Adjoining flats with a single interconnecting door,' H suggests.

'You two could meet up to decide when each of you will have me.'

'We could draw up a rota.'

'And sometimes when you are both fed up with me you'll allow me out or temporarily kick me out to screw somebody else. Because, you see, ultimately I'm a clever submissive. I want to be told what to do but only by someone clever enough to tell me to do what I want. And that somebody has to be a woman, one I consider wonderful, for no man tells me what to do because most of what men have created and continue to create is nonsensical.'

I continue to expound on my theory. 'People can be happy but all the great religious and moral traditions end up causing misery. Most of our institutions, far from helping, get in the way. The leadership of most politicians is self-serving because they are there only because they are dominant alpha types intent not on doing good but on proving their superiority – and they neither know it nor admit it.'

'Which means you'd better stand down from politics,' says H, wisely, 'because although you've successfully concealed all this for years now, you won't get away with it forever. At some stage, the shit is going to hit the fan.'

'Yes,' I say. 'I know it will. In which case, perhaps it might be fun to be the one to throw it!'